Involving young researchers

How to enable young people to
design and conduct research

Perpetua Kirby

The **Joseph Rowntree Foundation** has supported this project as part of its programme of research and innovative development projects, which it hopes will be of value to policy makers, practitioners and service users. The facts presented and views expressed in this report are, however, those of the author and not necessarily those of the Foundation.

A companion volume to *Involving young researchers* is published in February 2000 by Save the Children:

Young people as researchers: A learning resource pack
Steve Worrall

This publication provides adaptable training exercises and handouts for workers training young people to undertake social research. Topics covered include: setting aims and objectives; choosing and designing research methods; ethical issues; taking part in analysis and report writing; and learner needs, support and evaluation. The pack contains identified competencies, and a section on theoretical issues, which describes some of the influences behind current training practice.

Young people as researchers is a collection of useful exercises, rather than a unitary research training course. It is designed to be used alongside the manual *Involving young researchers*.

Price: £9.95
ISBN: 1 84187 011 0
(Published in February 2000 by Save the Children. Tel: 0171 703 5400)

© Joseph Rowntree Foundation 1999

All rights reserved.

Published for the Joseph Rowntree Foundation by YPS
in association with Save the Children

**This report is based primarily on work
with young researchers within Save the Children**

ISBN 1 902633 45 8

Cover illustrations by Angela Martin

Prepared and printed by:
York Publishing Services Ltd
64 Hallfield Road
Layerthorpe
York
YO31 7ZQ
Tel: 01904 430033 Fax: 01904 430868 E-mail: orders@yps.ymn.co.uk

Contents

Acknowledgements

I would particularly like to thank Bridget Pettitt, Clive Hedges and Paula Rodgers (Save the Children) for their continual support, advice and expertise whilst researching and writing this publication.

There are many staff within Save the Children who have considerable experience of involving young researchers and who have contributed to the development of this area of research. It is their practice and views that have helped to shape this report: Kieran Breen, Nicola Chapman, Julie Dobson, Sue Emerson, Goretti Horgan, Radhika Howarth, Maddy Lewis, Peter Little, Carol Nevison, Jonathan Oldham, Ciaran McKeown, Rachel Searle-Mbullu, Alan Siddall, Andy West. Their work can be found referenced within this report.

I am also very grateful to the following people in other organisations who shared their experience of working with young researchers: Mick Appleyard and Nichola King [Society of Volunteering Associates (SOVA)], Clare Hackett (Upper Springfield Development Trust), Ann Hobbiss (University of Bradford), Lindsey Collins and Sophie Laws (research consultant).

In addition, I would like to thank those who gave their time to read a draft copy of this report and offer their valuable comments: Dr Howard Williamson (Cardiff University); Pat Roach, Gill Henson and Mick Appleyard (SOVA); and Felicity Shenton (University of Durham). Also those within Save the Children: Chris Cuninghame, Kathryn Potter, Richard Morran, Elizabeth Morrison, Caroline Pook, Madeleine Tearse.

Save the Children is very grateful to Joseph Rowntree Foundation for recognising the importance of disseminating practice in this relatively unexplored area of research.

Most importantly, I would like to thank all the young researchers whose views and experiences have informed this report. I do not

know all their names – as many were interviewed confidentially –
so I am therefore unable to acknowledge everyone individually.
Their own research, which is referenced throughout this publication,
is a testament to their achievements.

Perpetua Kirby

Introduction

Respect for children and young people's views is enshrined in the UN Convention on the Rights of the Child (UNICEF 1995), ratified by the United Kingdom government in 1991. The best interests of the child should be taken into account, and children have the right to freedom of expression (Article 12) and the 'freedom to seek, receive and impart information and ideas of all kind' (Article 13).

There has been a growing movement to listen to children and young people, and research is one way in which they can have a say. Over the last couple of decades, there has been an expanding body of studies which examine the views and needs of children and young people. Participatory research methods have also been developed to enable them to better share their experiences and express their views.

As well as encouraging children and young people to participate more fully as research subjects, Save the Children and others (e.g. Alderson, 1995; Ash et al., 1996; Fast Forward Positive Lifestyles Ltd, 1994) have started to examine ways in which children and young people can be actively involved in conducting research. Save the Children alone has supported more than 25 research studies involving young researchers, in which they participated in all or some of the stages of research, from defining the research aims and methods to collecting and analysing the data.

Participatory research is not just about improved research methods. It is also about achieving democratic participation and social justice for children and young people. By influencing what is researched, and how their lives are represented, they participate in institutional decision-making processes. The more young people become actively engaged in research, the more they personally gain, and the more they may expect – and demand – that changes come out of the findings.

This publication demonstrates how young people can be competently and usefully involved in conducting research. Young researchers have primarily been involved in researching other young people, but they have also researched adults' views. The participation of young people in research is challenging, enjoyable and can be highly beneficial to all those involved. These projects take time, however, and sometimes evolve in unforeseen ways, responding as they do to the needs of the young people within each research context. There are no easy formulas to follow, but only ideas and the experience of others that can help to guide us:

> Often projects aimed at involving children in local decision making turn it into planning processes that use children as 'hostages' for adult interests. For children to really participate in planning requires something more than just asking them about their opinions. It takes an extended period of time, and means involving children and adults in an open-minded *process* in which no one knows the final outcome. (Chawla and Kjørholt, 1996, p. 43)

How was this book researched?

The ideas within this book are based on the experience and views of many adult researchers, youth and development workers, and young people. The perspectives of some other professionals – including researchers, statutory workers and funders – to research involving young people are also incorporated.

The contents of the book are based primarily on a large internal evaluation of seven Save the Children research projects involving young people (Kirby and Pettitt, 1998). The views of workers and young people involved in more than 15 other similar projects – both within and outside Save the Children – were also collected using interviews. Another important source of information was the research reports outlining research involving young people.

Who is the book for?

This publication is intended for practitioners who want to carry out, or commission, research involving young researchers. This includes professional researchers and academics, as well as others who work with young people and conduct research (e.g. schools, youth and voluntary agencies, and statutory departments).

It is assumed that the reader will already know about when and how to do research, or will be reading other texts on this subject. Some direction will be given to further references on the wider methodological and theoretical research issues. There is an accompanying set of learning resource materials to assist workers to train young people in research (Worrall, 2000). The report refers readers to this pack by indicating: ⊃ see Learning Resource Materials.

Which young people is the book about?

The emphasis here is primarily on involving young people aged 14 to 25 in research, although some of the cited studies have included younger children, including those as young as eight years. The young people involved in these projects were often disadvantaged; including those who had been in local authority care, excluded from school, the homeless, young mothers, refugees and those from minority ethnic groups. Most of the work cited was conducted in the United Kingdom, although some studies were undertaken overseas, and the issues raised can be applied to working with young people internationally.

The accompanying learning resource materials are aimed at training young people aged 14 to 21.

Terms of reference

This book explores the democratisation of research, in which adults do research *with* young people, rather than *on* them. The emphasis here is on how to involve young people in designing and conducting research; it is not a manual on participatory research methods used to collect data from young respondents.

Young people can participate in research in various ways; taking part in different stages of the process and having different levels of decision-making power (see section on 'Level of participation' in Chapter 2). This publication illustrates many ways of involving young people in research, and shares some of the lessons learned by others, but it does not offer prescriptive models of how to do participatory research.

The definitions of terms commonly used in this book are given in Table 1.

How to find your way through the book

Chapter 1: Deciding to involve young researchers

Explores how to decide whether to involve young people in conducting research.

Chapter 2: How young researchers can participate

Examines the different ways in which young researchers can participate in the research process; including the different stages of research and the different levels of decision-making power they can have.

Table 1 Definition of terms

Term	Definition
Young researchers	The young people involved in designing and/or conducting a piece of research.
Respondents	The people whose views are being researched. This includes both young people and adults, unless the text specifically refers to 'young respondents' or 'adult respondents'.
Young participants	All the young people involved in the research – either as researchers or respondents.
Peers	People who share similar experiences and status; such as age, ethnicity and area of residence. (See section on 'Defining the target group of young researchers' in Chapter 3.)
Participatory research	Research which involves young people in designing and/or conducting the process.
Participatory research methods	Child-centred research methods used to collect data from young people, which can be used by either adult or young researchers. Examples include observation, drama, role play, drawing, and video. (See section on 'Participatory research methods' in Chapter 4.)

Chapter 3: Setting up the project

Outlines important issues to consider when setting up a research project involving young people; including how to recruit young researchers, workers' roles, what support to offer, and ways to maintain their interest and motivation.

Chapter 4: Doing the research

Explores how to involve young researchers in the different stages of conducting the research; from introducing the research and setting the aims, through to choosing the methods and collecting the data.

Chapter 5: Analysis and write up

Examines how to involve young people in analysing research data and writing up the research findings.

Chapter 6: Ethics

Outlines the additional ethical issues involved when young people research the views of their peers; including dealing with disclosure and safety issues.

Chapter 7: Dissemination and development

Outlines ways of involving young people in the dissemination of the research, evaluating the research and in further development work.

1 Deciding to involve young researchers

If you are deciding whether to involve young people in conducting research, then it is likely that you are in one of the following positions:

- you want to conduct a piece of research, and you are interested in having young people participate in the research process, or

- you work participatively with young people – or want to – and you need to decide whether research might be one way of involving them, or

- your role is to educate young people – including teaching them about research – and you want to explore ways of doing so.

This decision needs careful consideration about *why* you want to involve young people in conducting research (see Table 2 for examples). Research is carried out for many different purposes, but there are three main reasons why you might want to involve young researchers.

- *Better research.* Involving young researchers can be a good method of collecting quality research data. It can also be a more ethical and democratic way of conducting research.

- *Participation.* Research is one way of involving young people as citizens. It increases their knowledge and access to decision-making structures, and enables them to take action for themselves.

- *Personal development.* The research experience increases the personal development of the young researchers themselves; helping them to gain knowledge, skills and confidence.

You may choose to emphasise one or a combination of these approaches, and your choice may be dependent on your own professional background. For example, academics may be more interested in this method as an ethical and improved way of conducting research, while professionals working in youth and statutory agencies may focus on increasing young people's participation, and those in schools or colleges may be more concerned about the educational possibilities for their students. While you may emphasise one reason over the others, it is important to take all three into account when working with young researchers.

This chapter examines a number of questions – listed in Table 3 – designed to help you decide whether to involve young people in research. The relevance of each of these questions to your project will depend on *why* you want to involve young researchers. It is worth looking at all the questions – but perhaps focusing more on those that are most relevant to your project. Only after having given them some thought is it advisable to plan *how* to involve young researchers.

Is the research necessary?

Is the research topic worthwhile?

As with all research, you have to think about whether the research topic is worth investigating (see Alderson, 1995). Do you need to do the research to find out what you want to know, or is the information already available elsewhere (e.g. existing research reports, agencies' monitoring statistics, minutes of meetings)? Certain communities – particularly those considered disadvantaged or 'deviant' – are often over-researched, and people can become wary of taking part in research as they know from experience that little might change for them as a result.

Table 2 Hypothetical examples of why workers want to involve young researchers

Professional group	Reasons for involving young people in research
Local authority	A local authority department wants to undertake an important piece of research into the needs of young people in the local area. They want good quality data to inform future practice. They would like to involve young people in helping to conduct the research to give them the opportunity to participate and to develop their own skills. It is also hoped that the young researchers will be able to find young people who are not in contact with services, to be included in the research.
Youth workers	A youth worker wants to support a group of young people to present their views about local services to professionals. They feel that research could be a good way for the group to take action, to develop their own skills and to find out the views of many other young people as well.
Academic researcher	An academic wants to carry out some in-depth research about the lives of young people. They are primarily concerned with ensuring the research is rigorously carried out and will stand up to academic criticism. They think young people will improve the research by helping to design appropriate interview questions and by making respondents feel more relaxed in interview situations.
Voluntary organisation	An organisation wants to evaluate its own services for young people. They want to involve the young people in decisions that affect them. They hope that by involving young researchers this will also encourage young people to be respondents, and will help to ensure the service users are more willing to accept any changes that the organisation makes as a result of the research.

What information is required and how will it be used?

To decide whether the research is necessary, it is important to be clear about why the research is being carried out; including the type of information required, how you plan to use it, and how the findings will benefit young people (see the following checklists).

Table 3 Questions to consider when deciding to involve young researchers

Question	Issues to be considered
Is the research necessary? (see p. 8)	Is the research topic worthwhile? What information is required and how will it be used? Would other methods of working be more appropriate?
Why should young people get involved? (see p. 12)	Do young people want to get involved? How will young people benefit from taking part?
How will the research differ if young researchers are involved? (see p. 16)	Will involving young researchers improve the quality of the research? Will young researchers have better access to those being researched? Will young researchers improve the validity of the research? What are the possible problems of involving young researchers? Is it suitable to involve young researchers in sensitive research topics? Should young people always research their own community? Should young people research adults' views? Will there be added benefits to involving young researchers?
Do you have the necessary resources? (see p. 29)	Do you have the necessary funds? Do you have the necessary time? Do you have access to young people? Do workers have the required skills?

What information do you require?

- Increase knowledge and develop theories: find out about people's lives, experiences and perceptions.

- Needs assessment: find out people's views and experiences, to identify unmet need.

- Evaluate your own service: identify good practice, and examine how your practice may be improved.

- Evaluate other services: identify good practice, and examine how others' practice may be improved.

- Evaluate proposed services/policies: find out what people think of the proposals.

- Monitor who uses services.

How will you use the information?

- Change your own services/policies.

- Develop new services.

- Campaign for changes to other agencies' services/policies.

- Inform others of young people's views and experiences.

- As evidence to get funds for services.

- Identify further research.

- Promote participation, by using the research as an example of how young people can participate in decision making.

- As evidence that the young researchers have learned research skills (possibly for accreditation).

Would other methods of working be more appropriate?

It might be that you do not need to do research and that other methods of involving young people may be more appropriate. The following check-lists are provided to help you make this decision.

Consider doing research if the following apply

- You need to find out the views or experiences of young people, and want to use a recognised and rigorous research methodology to ensure you represent these views accurately.

- It is important to demonstrate that you have accurately represented the views of young people.

- The research will produce usable findings which incorporate the views of all those consulted.

- You expect the research to have a greater impact than just a successful process for the young researchers themselves.

- You or others plan to disseminate or act upon the research findings, so that the participating young people will not feel let down.

Consider other methods of working if the following apply

- The desired information can be obtained from just a few young people – perhaps an established group you can easily access or those you already work with.

- Other methods can have the same or better desired outcomes.

- The sole concerns are to increase young people's participation and build their personal development, rather than act upon research findings.

Why should young people get involved?

Do young people want to get involved?

Some groups of young people may decide themselves that they want to do research, and the question then is whether you can support them to do the work. If the research idea comes from adults, it is particularly important to consider what will motivate the young people to take part (see sections on 'Maintaining motivation and interest' in Chapter 3 and 'Setting aims and objectives' in Chapter 4). Some important factors which can affect their motivation include:

- whether they are interested in the research topic and whether it is relevant to their own lives

- how they will personally benefit (see section on 'How will young people benefit from taking part?' later in this chapter)

- how it will help their community

- how much time they will need to spend

- the level of support offered.

> I want to do something so that my brothers and sisters do not suffer the way I did. (Young researcher, quoted in Howarth, 1997)

The young researchers' reasons for doing the research may well be different from your own and partner agencies may also have other reasons for getting involved. As with any partnership, this is worth exploring in advance. Adult researchers in one project highlighted the difficulty of managing the different stakeholders' agendas:

> The team [of young researchers] had very little experience of research except as previous subjects of research, and we began by seeing young people as participating in 'our' research and that we needed to devolve ownership during the course of the project. Neither of us [adults] saw ourselves as participating as researchers in 'their' campaign to improve other young people's lives – although this was our shared overall aspiration. (Hobbiss *et al.*, 1998a, p. 5)

It is equally important to ensure that young people are not forced to participate. Workers should be careful not to introduce participatory research as a way of working when the young people do not want to take part or would rather be involved in other kinds of projects, particularly those that are more fun. Case study 1 illustrates that young people are not always interested in doing research suggested by adults.

Case study 1 Young people's social and leisure needs in central Coventry

Youth workers in the centre of Coventry had seen a research report produced by a neighbouring group of young researchers. The workers tried to set up a similar small-scale peer research project in their own local area, looking at young people's social and leisure needs. The workers, and a couple of experienced young researchers from the neighbouring area, organised an initial group discussion with 15 young people, but found that none was interested in doing the research. The workers had to undertake the research themselves. Reasons given for the lack of interest included:

- young people questioned the need for the research as a leisure centre was already being planned locally

- young people felt let down by the recent closure of a youth club night

- young people took little pride in their local area, and they typically used leisure services and other resources outside the area

- the offer of £200 for group activities was not considered enough personal incentive (Oldham, 1998).

How will young people benefit from taking part?

Young researchers have been found to get a lot out of taking part in research projects, primarily their own personal development (e.g. Precht, 1998) (see Table 4). They also welcome the opportunity to have their views heard and to help others in their community. Another important motivator for them is the social aspects of the project. Where they are paid for their work, this income is clearly a major incentive for some young people, although sometimes payment can interfere with their welfare benefits (see section on 'Paying young researchers' in Chapter 3). Their research experience can also lead on to further employment and education opportunities.

For the young people to benefit from the research, the workers need to offer considerable individual and group support, and make the project fun. Otherwise young people may easily get bored and lose motivation (see sections on 'Support' and 'Maintaining motivation and interest' in Chapter 3).

Table 4 Ways in which young people can benefit from being young researchers

Benefits	The main advantages
Improved citizenship	Local ownership of the research. Opportunity to have a say in local planning and decision-making processes. An opportunity to help their community. Enhanced knowledge of the community and decision-making structures. 'We don't get told where the funding goes and where they get it from. We got to go to [various local] meetings, things that we didn't even know that happened. But we get involved in these things now' (young researcher, quoted in Kirby and Pettitt, 1998).
Personal development (see section on 'Support' in Chapter 3)	Personal confidence particularly improves; including working in a group, and speaking to people they do not know and those in authority. Skills: for example, group work, listening, literacy, numeracy, computing, building relationships, interpersonal communication, non-judgemental understanding. Knowledge: including research methodology, background policy and information, decision-making structures, understanding of people and community issues. Experience of research and working in a team. Sense of self-worth and identity. Networking: developing personal contacts and establishing a dialogue with adults.
Social (see section on 'Maintaining motivation and interest' in Chapter 3)	Meeting people. Making friends. Having fun. Social events.
Reimbursement/ recognition (see sections on 'Paying young researchers' and 'Support' in Chapter 3)	Payment. Food. Outings. Certificate of achievement. Authored research report.
Future opportunities (see section on 'Support' in Chapter 3)	Improved job opportunities, by increasing confidence, and providing work experience and a reference. Can influence their future plans to go on to further education, employment or community work. 'I've got a lot out of doing [the research], more confidence, in job interviews saying I can do this' (young researcher, quoted in Kirby and Pettitt, 1998).

How will the research differ if young researchers are involved?

Will involving young researchers improve the quality of the research?

The quality of research carried out by young researchers can achieve a high standard. Involving young researchers will not in itself increase the voice of the individuals being researched, however. The participation of the young researchers needs to be balanced with quality controls to ensure the data are meaningful and useful, reflecting the views of all the young people (and adults) the research claims to represent.

There are debates about what is 'good' research, and the criteria by which people judge quality are different (for review of different research perspectives, see Trinder, 1996). For example, quantitative researchers will look for a large and representative sample, and those using qualitative research may be more concerned with the depth of information collected. It is important to consider which criteria your research is going to be measured against – depending on who is your intended audience and which research methodology you use – and that you address these issues.

The quality of this type of participatory research is often related to whether the workers and young researchers place a greater emphasis on the aim of doing a good piece of research, or more on the participation and personal development of the researchers.

Will young researchers have better access to those being researched?

Young people can find it easier than adult researchers to get in contact with other young people. They have access to their network

> **Case study 2 Bangladeshi young people's access to further education**
>
> One study examined the participation of Bangladeshi young people in a further education (FE) college, including why some drop out. The FE college being studied did not have the names of those who had left, and the only way to access these young people therefore was to snowball out into the community, asking friends of friends whether they had dropped out of the college. Young researchers recruited from the local Bangladeshi community were best placed to do this (Howarth, forthcoming).

of friends, and can 'snowball' out to friends of their friends, to reach a wider group of young people (see Case study 2). This can help to include typically hard to find respondents in the sample – particularly those who are not in contact with services – although this will depend on the type of young researchers doing the research (see Arber, 1993).

Most groups of young researchers have difficulty finding a sufficiently representative group of young people to include in their research by snowball sampling alone. They also sometimes lack the confidence to approach others their age if they do not already know them, without additional training and worker support.

In many instances, they will need to access young people, and adults, through other professional agencies. Here, they often face the same – and sometimes more – problems getting past gate keepers (e.g. school teachers or social workers) than adult researchers (e.g. Alderson, 1995; Booth *et al.*, 1998) (see section on 'Accessing respondents' in Chapter 4). This will vary depending on the extent to which professionals consider the issue being investigated is sensitive or contentious. Access can be harder still in agencies with ethics committees (see section on 'Research ethics committees' in Chapter 6).

Will young researchers improve the validity of the research?

The young researchers' status within their community can enable them to improve the validity (i.e. accuracy) of the collected data. Their insider knowledge of the issues being studied, and of the community being researched, has been found to be highly valuable in the following ways (see Chapter 4 on 'Doing the research' and Chapter 5 on 'Analysis and write up'):

- designing appropriate research tools

- eliciting information from others

- interpreting what people say.

When researching young people, using young researchers helps to reduce the power imbalance between the researcher and respondents (for more information, see 'Power in research' box). For example, young people may better understand each others' language and the young respondents may feel less intimidated by young researchers. Involving young researchers also helps to ensure the issues most relevant to young people are identified and addressed by the research.

The peer researchers' age and a combination of other factors (listed in Table 5) can help to make the research setting less formal; enabling the respondents to be more relaxed and thus more open (see Case study 3):

> In one instance a silent class of teenage girls became a room of buzzing conversation when the student researchers took over the session from the adult co-ordinator and met with the girls in small groups to discuss their views on tourism. (Precht, 1998, p. 40)

Case study 3 Drug use in Lothian

In the Fast Forward Positive Lifestyles Ltd (1994) study of drug use amongst 12 to 16 year olds in Lothian, they found the 'fresh approach' of using young researchers aged 18 to 25 meant the setting was more informal than having a professional adult researcher:

The focus of discussion in research sessions usually moved naturally but perceptively away from the worker, and over to the less formally spoken [young researchers] volunteers … whether due to age, use of language or perceived similar experience on the part of the volunteers – and normally a combination of these qualities (none is necessarily sufficient – alone), the young people were quicker to relax, seemed more comfortable and were happier to talk about sensitive issues without fear of reprisal. The interaction is more natural. (p. 9)

Power in research: *Read on if you want to know more …*

Ideas on the reduction of power in participatory research extend from the symbolic interactionist perspective in which the respondent's account is, in part, a function of the interview, and meanings are negotiated between the researcher and those being researched. Feminist research has also attempted to develop ways in which to reduce any hierarchy between the researcher and those being researched, to improve the dialogue between the two (see Oakley, 1981; Olesen, 1998; Schwandt, 1998).

What are the possible problems of involving young researchers?

Young researchers can still experience some of the same problems adult researchers face when researching young people. Setting up a formal research situation – such as an interview – can shift the researcher–researched relationship so that the young researchers are no longer perceived just as 'peers', but they also attain the status of being a 'researcher'. Some of the problems young researchers have encountered are illustrated in Table 6. There is no reason to believe that they experience these problems any more than adult researchers; indeed, their age suggests they are likely to happen less frequently.

Table 5 Factors that help young researchers to gain improved data from respondents

Factor	Reason for importance
Age	Young people are often deferential to those who are older – and more so in certain cultures – which can lead them to tell adults what they believe is expected. Talking to those closer in age makes the setting more informal and relaxed, and can help respondents to say what they really think.
Speaking a common language	Within a language there are different local shared references and meanings associated with words. An understanding of these is important when conducting research and something young peers can offer. They can also input their knowledge of the local language – by helping to construct the questions and interpret respondents' comments – without necessarily having to conduct the interviews. 'Where the worker talked about temazepam, the [young researcher] volunteers could talk about Norrie 10s or 20s (the brand name is Normison)' (Fast Forward Positive Lifestyles Ltd, 1994, p. 9).
Knowing others	Young researchers can often persuade friends and acquaintances within their community to take part in the research, and encourage them to be more open. The young researchers can also use their knowledge of these respondents' lives to probe for more information.
Sharing common experiences	If researchers have shared experiences and specialised knowledge of those being researched, this helps them to identify the issues to research, to 'relate' to what people talk about and empathise by 'knowing how they felt', all of which can help to probe further.
Being on the same side	In some projects, it has been considered important that the local researchers were seen 'to be on the same side' as those they were interviewing, as this enabled them to have greater access to information. Young researchers do not always empathise with those from their own community, however, and may require additional training to do so (see sections on 'Conducting face to face research methods' in Chapter 4; 'Level of interpretation' in Chapter 5; and 'The ethics of involving young researchers' in Chapter 6).

Continued

Table 5 Factors that help young researchers to gain improved data from respondents (continued)

Factor	Reason for importance
Taboo topics	Some subjects may be more taboo for young people to talk about with adults than with others their age. In such instances, it may be particularly beneficial to use young researchers. For example, adult researchers are exploring young people's perceptions of security in the United Kingdom, Germany and Russia, which is an abstract subject, and one which can be particularly taboo in some regions. They are involving young researchers to facilitate focus group discussions to help break down the power differential between respondents and interviewer, and to help overcome the sensitivity of this subject matter (Webber and Longhurst, forthcoming).

Table 6 Ways in which young researchers experience similar problems to adult researchers

Problem	The main issues
Status	The young researchers' 'status' and 'authority' as researchers sometimes align them more with outsiders of the community than as insiders. This can be offset, somewhat, if the research setting is made less formal.
	Young Researcher I: 'Once you open up the interview you become part of the authority, and it's completely weird … you think you are just like them but when they answer the questions they are defensive and think you are the law and authority.'
	Young Researcher II: 'Even if you know things about them, it was really surprising, they look at you differently, as part of the institution, but the whole idea of the research was that we were [from the local community]' (quoted in Kirby and Pettitt, 1998).
Lack of interest	Young researchers also find that some interviewees are uninterested in the research interview (e.g. Precht, 1998; Saunders and Broad, 1997).
Biased replies	As in all research, some young researchers have also reported that young respondents sometimes say what

Continued

Table 6 Ways in which young researchers experience similar problems to adult researchers (continued)

Problem	The main issues
	they think is expected of them, rather than what they actually truly believe (Precht, 1998).
Self-completion questionnaires	This research method is notorious for having a low response rate, and there is no evidence to suggest that this is any different when distributed by young peers. For example, one postal survey of 663 households had only a 19 per cent response rate (Connolly *et al.*, 1996).

The degree to which different interviewers – including peers – impact on the respondents' accounts has not yet been sufficiently investigated, and there is also an absence of research which asks young respondents who they would like to be interviewed by, and how this is affected by the topic being researched. This is an area workers and young people might want to include in future studies.

There is some evidence from within Save the Children that young people do not always want to be interviewed by their own peers. For example, workers held a discussion with one group of young people, and asked them whether they would prefer to be interviewed by young people or adults. The boys typically did not want to be interviewed by their peers because they believed research conducted by young researchers would not be taken seriously and would not have an impact. The girls were more likely to want to talk to someone their own age.

Is it suitable to involve young researchers in sensitive research topics?

There is some evidence to suggest that when talking about sensitive issues some young people may be less willing to talk to their peers – particularly those they know or will see around. Instead, they may prefer to talk to an independent 'professional' with a clearly defined role which ensures their anonymity and confidentiality in these circumstances. For example, young researchers interviewing others about leaving care said it had been a disadvantage to interview those they would see again because this meant the respondents 'didn't fully open up' (Saunders and Broad, 1997, p. 65). (Also see literature on children and young people seeking advice or help, for example: Archbold *et al.*, 1998; Boldero and Fallown, 1995; Westcott and Davies, 1995.)

People find some subjects particularly difficult to talk about, regardless of whether the researcher is an adult or young person; for example, a young researcher mentioned that a girl had been 'embarrassed' talking about her intestinal surgery (Alderson, 1995). With other subjects, young people may feel less willing to open up to someone their age if they feel they will be judged by them. In one project, the young researchers felt others were unwilling to admit that they had been bullied (HAYS and Kirby, 1998).

Discussing sensitive research issues can raise painful issues for the young researchers (see section on 'Disclosure of sensitive information' in Chapter 6). As a result, young researchers have sometimes moved the interview on past difficult topics of discussion, rather than probe for more information.

> Some of the things the [young] interviewers were told affected them, brought certain things up for them, and they found it hard to just swallow their feelings and carry on. (Saunders and Broad, 1997, p. 65)

Should young people always research their own community?

The involvement of people in decisions affecting their lives is one of the underlying principles of participatory research, and often why the young people affected by research are recruited to be researchers.

Some research lends itself automatically to the inclusion of young researchers because of the topic being studied. Studies that explore ways in which young people participate within organisations, for example, are clear candidates for involving young researchers in their design and implementation (see Nevison, 1996; Save the Children and Whitley Abbey School, 1999).

When undertaking this type of participatory research, it is necessary to carefully decide which young people are involved as young researchers in each project – first considering who is a peer or from the same community. This will depend on the subject of the research, how the community is defined, and in what way the findings are to be used (see section on 'Recruiting young researchers' in Chapter 3). It can be tempting to encourage the participation of any young people as young researchers, even if they are not from the community concerned, as demonstrated by Case study 4.

In some projects, however, researchers from outside the community may be better placed to undertake the research, for the following reasons.

- *Collect differing views.* If researching a wide community, outsider researchers may be best placed to collect the many differing and competing views within the community, as they will not be identified with any community sub-groups. For example, Naples (1997) found it an advantage being an outside researcher when studying adults in rural Iowa:

  My own 'outsiderness' became a resource through which I was able to acquire an 'insider' perspective on many residents' perception of alienation from others in the community. (Naples, 1997, p. 71)

Case study 4 Pupils' participation in school

A group of young researchers conducted a piece of research in their own local community, and a head teacher in a neighbouring area invited them to conduct some research on how young people could better participate in the running of his school. It was felt, however, that the group of young researchers were not peers of those in the school – as they were no longer at school, some had been permanently excluded or had left school at an early age, and they lived in a different part of the city. It was decided that it was more important to encourage the children and young people in the school to undertake their own research. A couple of the experienced young researchers helped workers to train the new group of school pupils to be researchers (Save the Children and Whitley Abbey School, 1999).

- *Probe for explanations.* Those with different experiences may sometimes be able to encourage research respondents to describe their views and daily life in greater detail than researchers who have shared experiences (Woodward and Chisholm, 1981) (see section on 'Conducting face to face research methods' in Chapter 4). For example, in one project, it was felt that peers had not probed deeply because they believed they already knew what was going to be said, or because they felt awkward asking the interviewees questions that they already knew the answer to (Kirby and Pettitt, 1998).

- *Maintaining distance.* Some researchers who are personally involved in a research topic may have biases which they are unable to suspend – or they will be perceived to be biased by others – in which case an independent outsider might be better placed to do the research.

- *Dangerous research subjects.* Some communities may not be supportive and nurturing, and for some people – such as sex workers and drug users – it could be particularly dangerous for them to confide to others from their own community.

If outsiders do conduct the research, the researchers can still be young people and from the same wider community as the respondents, as illustrated in Case study 5.

Case study 5 Bangladeshi young people's access to further education

Young researchers recruited to examine the participation of Bangladeshi young people in a further education college were selected from the local Bangladeshi community, but they were not students at the college being researched. It was felt that, if they were not students there, this would help to ensure they did not bias the research through personal experiences of the college. It was also thought that by being more independent the findings could then be published and would be treated more seriously (Howarth, forthcoming).

Should young people research adults' views?

Adults impact greatly on young people's lives, and young researchers can be involved in researching adults' views. Sometimes, young researchers may focus on adults alone (e.g. Nevison, 1996), or they may research adults and young people (e.g. HAYS and Kirby, 1998). Research about children and young people can be enhanced if it also examines the views of adults – such as professionals, parents, community leaders, neighbours, shop keepers, etc. This promotes a dialogue between them and young people, and helps to understand the different perspective on issues affecting young people. If the aim of the project is for young people to hold professionals accountable for their work, then it may also be considered appropriate for them to interview adults (for example, see Nevison, 1996).

When deciding whether young or adult researchers should interview adults, take into account the following issues (see section on 'Face to face contact with adult respondents' in Chapter 4).

* Adults may feel intimidated by the young researchers, and may be more open with an adult researcher.

* Young researchers can find it more difficult to probe adults, because of the power imbalance and because adults often use jargon and unfamiliar words.

Case study 6 National study of young people's experience of leaving care

Young researchers (aged 16 to 25) – who had themselves experienced care – researched the needs of young people leaving care across England. They conducted interviews with young people, and also a number of professionals working with those leaving care. Some local authority and voluntary agencies would not let them interview workers about their work. Some of those who did agree to be interviewed appeared to do so under duress, and others 'were not prepared to take seriously the interview process with young people, claiming the questions were not answerable or that the interview would take too long' (West, 1997).

- Some adult professionals may not take young researchers seriously, particularly if they have a professional relationship – such as 'teacher–student' or 'social worker–care leaver' – as illustrated in Case study 6.

If adults are to be interviewed by workers – rather than young researchers – young people can still be consulted about what questions to ask the adult respondents and can help to design the research project.

Will there be added benefits to involving young researchers?

Involving young researchers has the added benefits of improving young people's access to decision making, holding adult researchers accountable, and of being egalitarian. It therefore challenges the wider structural inequalities that young people face in society, and demonstrates their ability to participate (for more information see 'Challenging power' box). This is reflected well by a professional's response in an evaluation of research conducted by young refugees (HAYS and Kirby, 1998):

A great advantage [involving young researchers] – it gave a clear message that young refugees have their own voice and can be active in developing good practice rather than being passive recipients of other people's ideas.

Challenging power: *Read on if you want to know more ...*

Feminist researchers have critiqued traditional research because it typically replicates wider structural hierarchies between professionals and those in socially less powerful positions, rather than trying to challenge these imbalances (for review, see Olesen, 1998). They have therefore attempted to define additional criteria of research adequacy and credibility – which address the power dynamics in the research context – rather than simple measures of validity typically used in research.

Child-focused research similarly needs to consider the extent to which it challenges – or replicates – the professionals' position of power over children and young people. Hobbiss *et al.* (1998a), for example, expressed the need for 'added value' measures when assessing the quality of young peer research, such as egalitarianism, shared ownership and equal opportunities to participate.

In addition, peer research enables young people to speak to their peers about their shared experiences, encouraging dialogue about these and enabling them to take joint action to change their lives (see Ash *et al.*, 1996, pp. 40–1). The young researchers can also act as role models for their peers – demonstrating what young people can do and how their contribution can be taken seriously by adults (e.g. Precht, 1998).

Participatory research is also part of a participatory learning approach, in which professionals share their knowledge and facilitate the group's critical awareness (Martin, 1996). Young researchers have been found to change their behaviour as a result of the information learned during the training in a research project. For example, a project on eco-tourism resulted in the young researchers no longer littering, telling others to protect the environment and noticing what impacts on their surroundings (Precht, 1998).

Do you have the necessary resources?

Do you have the necessary funds?

Involving young researchers is a relatively expensive way of doing research as it takes a considerable amount of worker and young researcher time (illustrated in the two sample timetables later in this chapter). It should not therefore be thought of as a fast and cheap alternative to 'professional' research. Participatory research does have a number of added benefits, however, as explored in the previous section. If the quality of the research is not high, it makes the method of research particularly expensive – and less cost effective – because the research is of less use to inform practice and campaign for change.

There are a number of possible costs listed. If you intend to work with young people with disabilities this may incur a number of additional costs.

The costs to consider are:

- worker costs (including recruitment, training, etc.)

- consultant costs (if required for specific training, advice, tasks)

- young researchers' costs (salary or other incentives, recruitment, training)

- compensation for research respondents

- residentials, social activities, food

- travel

- child care

- training equipment (e.g. flip charts, pens, adhesive, etc.)

- research equipment (e.g. tape recorders, videos, tapes, batteries, computer software)

- hire of venue (for training and research meetings)

- interpretation, translation

- background research literature (subscriptions, publications)

- stationery and photocopying (could be extensive if use questionnaires)

- design and print of research reports

- production of other products (e.g. leaflets, posters, videos, etc.)

- launch event (e.g. hire of venue, invitations, delegate packs, refreshments)

- postage (including disseminating the reports)

- telephone

- transcription.

Possible additional costs if working with a group with physical or sensory disabilities include:

- transport to all meetings

- interpretation

- specialist workers

- carers (for residentials).

Do you have the necessary time?

Undertaking participatory research with young researchers takes considerable time. Realistic planning is needed to calculate the number of hours to be spent on the different stages of the research for each project. This will depend on the research brief and the needs of the young people in the group. Projects require different levels of input, as illustrated in the two sample timetables later in this chapter. The amount of time spent by workers and young researchers depends on a number of factors, as follows.

- *Type of participation.* More time is required the more participatory the project and the more the young researchers are involved in making decisions and taking part in the different stages of the research process (see Chapter 2 on 'How young researchers can participate').

- *Scale and quality of the research.* More work is required on larger scale projects and when the quality of the research is a main aim. For example, it takes longer to produce a long and detailed final report than just a brief summary of research findings (see section on 'Will involving young researchers improve the quality of the research?' earlier in this chapter).

- *Recruitment.* If young researchers need to be recruited to join the research project, this takes considerable worker time (see section on 'Recruiting young researchers' in Chapter 3).

- *Training and support.* Considerable time is needed to prepare young people to become involved in research. Projects which offer more support – including additional training on research-related issues – require more time (see section on 'Support' in Chapter 3).

- *Researchers' needs.* Groups require varying levels of worker support, depending on the young researchers' individual needs (see section on 'Support' in Chapter 3).

- *Group work support.* Some projects offer more group work support to the researchers. This tends to result in the groups continuing to work after the end of the research – setting up further projects or youth forums of their own (see section on 'Future development work with young researchers' in Chapter 7).

- *Administration.* These projects can entail large amounts of administrative work, particularly when young people are paid and need support with time sheets, bank accounts, benefit issues, etc.

- *Conferences and presentations.* Young researchers often get invited to conferences or local policy meetings to present their research and discuss their own views about a given subject. These meetings are extremely beneficial to the group – helping to build their confidence and to recognise the value of their opinions and expertise – but require additional time and preparation support.

Note that young researchers are frequently unable – or unwilling – to do additional work in their own time, and most work should be planned to take place during arranged meetings.

Sample timetable 1 Education support needs of young refugees

A group of young refugees (aged 16 to 21) was recruited to research a refugee issue of their choice in west London. The group – called HAYS (Horn of Africa Youth Scheme) – decided to research the educational support needs of local refugees from the Horn of Africa. They were supported by a research trainer, a youth worker, and another project worker who also undertook the necessary administrative duties (HAYS and Kirby, 1998).

Time spent on the project

Workers' hours (excluding development work): approximately 2,000 hours.

Seven young researchers' hours (paid): approximately 800 hours.

Mar. – Apr. 1997	Set up advisory group and recruit youth worker.
May	Outreach to youth and community groups, and advertise using leaflets and posters.
July	Recruit young people: had to wait for some young people to finish exams.
Aug.	30 hours' training in the holidays; included research issues, relevant policy, interpretation and local authority structures.

Sept. – Oct.	Planning: the group found it hard to meet because of college commitments. Considerable time spent deciding which issue to research; long time developing interview schedule together with the research worker.
Oct. – Dec.	Fieldwork: harder than anticipated to find 34 young people who would be interviewed. Time needed to negotiate access to schools/colleges.
Dec. 1997 – Jan. 1998	Analysis: the group spent a weekend coding the data. The research worker then completed the analysis, and discussed this with the group.
Feb. – Mar.	Report: the research worker wrote most of the report but consulted the group and advisory group about content. Two young researchers wrote a section of the report, and the group commented on the final draft.
Mar. – Apr.	Design report: a professional designer designed the summary report. A full report was also produced, but not professionally designed.
April	Launch: presentation made by the young researchers at launch attended by professionals and young people.
April – July	Dissemination: to national and local agencies, and the youth press.
May 1998 – Mar. 1999	Development work: attend conferences, set up refugee youth forum, campaign to implement recommendations, etc. Translation: summary findings published in four different refugee community languages.

Sample timetable 2 Pupils' participation in school

Research was conducted on how young people could better participate in the running of their school. Two youth workers worked with a total of 22 pupils from the school, in smaller groups. Using a range of research methods, they asked their opinions about the school. They also supported a core group of ten of these young people to be researchers and to design their own research methods to use with their fellow pupils. The views of the initial group, and of the other young pupils they researched, were all incorporated into the final report.

A couple of experienced young researchers from a neighbouring area helped two youth workers to train the new group of young researchers in the school. Two adult researchers advised and supported the youth workers throughout the project. A designated teacher liaised between the youth workers and the school. An adult researcher interviewed teachers about how they thought the pupils could participate in the school (Save the Children and Whitley Abbey School, 1999).

Time spent on the project

Workers and experienced young researchers (excluding development work): approximately 950 hours.

Core group of ten young pupil researchers (voluntary): approximately 716 hours.

July–Aug. 1998	Four partner agencies make agreement.
Sept.	Inform school year assemblies about the project.
Oct.–Nov.	Have weekly meetings with 22 interested young people (around 12 attending at any one meeting) to ask their views about how they could participate more in the school. Workers demonstrated a range of research methods by using these to collect the young researchers' own views about the school.
Dec.	Residential: to explore which research methods the group could use themselves to ask the views of other young people in the school. They chose role plays, self-completion questionnaires and group discussions.
Dec.	Meetings to design research tools.
Jan. 1999	Finalise research tools.
Jan.–Feb.	The young researchers undertake their own research with other pupils in the school.
	Adult researcher conducts interviews with teachers and other school staff.

Feb.–Mar.	Analysis by workers in consultation with the young pupil researchers.
Apr.	Report on young people's findings written by workers.
May–June	Dissemination: report disseminated in the school. Young people produce a poster of their findings and make presentations at school assemblies.
Apr.–July	Development work with the young pupil researchers and other pupils: implement findings with the school council and teachers.
Sept.	Full report completed by workers, including both pupils' and teachers' views and an evaluation of the project.

Do you have access to young people?

If you already work with young people, then you will have access to potential young researchers. Otherwise you will need to find an established group to work with or recruit a new group, which can take time (see section on 'Recruiting young researchers' in Chapter 3).

Another important factor to assess is whether those young people available to take part have the capacities required for the research project. If not, can workers help the young people to participate by finding the additional resources needed, such as longer timescales, extra workers, further training, etc.? (see sections on 'Recruiting young researchers' and 'Support' in Chapter 3).

Do workers have the required skills?

Assess whether your team has the necessary research, youth work and administrative skills to undertake a research project with young researchers (see section on 'Roles of young researchers and workers' in Chapter 3). If young people with particular support needs – including low literacy levels or disabilities – are involved then additional worker skills may be required. Where you do not have the required skills in-house, then you may need to add the cost of buying in other workers.

KEY LEARNING POINTS: Deciding to involve young researchers

- Young people are involved in research for three main reasons: to improve the research, to increase young people's participation in society, and to improve their own personal development. All three need careful consideration.

- Before deciding to do research with young people consider whether the research topic is worthwhile, what information is required, how this will be used, and how it will benefit young people. It may be that other methods of participatory working would be more appropriate than research to achieve your intended outcomes.

- Young people usually get a lot out of doing research, but some will not want to participate. Young researchers can gain many personal benefits, if they are appropriately supported by workers.

- Quality controls are important to ensuring the quality of participatory research.

- Whilst young researchers often have access to many other young people, they usually also have to find respondents through other agencies.

- Young researchers can help to improve the accuracy of data collected from young respondents, by enabling them to be more relaxed and open up, although some still experience similar problems to adult researchers. Young interviewees do not always want to be interviewed by other young researchers, particularly when the research subject is sensitive.

- When young people research their own communities, it is important to define what is meant by community and which young people should be involved as researchers. Sometimes, those from outside a community are better placed to research the different views of those within it.

- Young people can also research adults' views, but consider how comfortable both the young researchers and adult respondents will feel in this situation.

- There are a number of added benefits to involving young researchers. These include the involvement of young people in decision-making processes, developing their critical awareness and challenging the inequalities that they face within society.

- Involving young researchers is expensive, requiring a lot of worker time and additional costs. The time needed will depend on a number of factors, including how much the young people participate in the research and the level of support they require.

- Consider whether you have access to young people who can take part in the research, and if workers have the necessary range of skills to support them.

2 How young researchers can participate

Once you have decided to involve young researchers, you need to consider *how* they will participate in the research process. This includes at what stage they will be involved and the extent to which they will have the power to make decisions at each stage.

Young researchers can take part in research in different ways, having varying degrees of control over the process. This may depend on your approach to the work; as a piece of research, participation or personal development. For example, in adult-led research studies, the young people often fulfil an advisory role about how the research should be designed, although sometimes they make joint decisions and even carry out some data collection. Other projects are set up to support young people to carry out their own research projects, in which they make all or most of the decisions and carry out the data collection.

Different stages of the research process

There are many stages within the research process (listed below), and research is often just one stage in ongoing development work. Within Save the Children, young people have been most frequently absent from certain parts of the research process – particularly setting the research agenda (commissioning and deciding the research topic) and analysing the collected information – often because it can be more difficult to involve them in these stages (see sections on 'Setting aims and objectives' in Chapter 4 and 'Analysing data' in Chapter 5).

The stages in the research process are:

- commission/initiate research

- set budgets

- decide the research topic

- set aims and objectives

- recruit researchers/other workers

- advisory/reference group

- choose research methods

- write research questions

- collect information (fieldwork)
    - young people's data
    - professionals' data
    - community adults' data
    - secondary data

- provide research data (i.e. own views/experience)

- analysis

- choose recommendations

- write report

- authorship

- produce other mediums (e.g. videos, posters, etc.)

- disseminate research findings

- access to research findings

- development and campaigning.

It is necessary to decide at which stages of the research young people will be involved – taking into account the time and commitment implications this will have for both workers and young people. Where possible, this decision is best discussed with the young people, and may be constantly negotiated throughout the project.

Level of participation

There are different ways in which young people can participate in the various stages of research. It needs to be clear what level of involvement the young researchers will have at each stage of the research process. An adapted version of Alderson and Montgomery's (1996) stages of participation in decision making is used below to illustrate the different ways in which young researchers can take part. This is not a hierarchy of participation, but a description of the different ways of involving young people at each stage of the research process.

1 *Being informed.* Young people are informed about research being carried out by others. This can include being told who commissioned the research, why and how it is being carried out, what it will be used for, and how they can get a copy of the research findings.

2 *Expressing a view.* Young people can express their views and experiences as research respondents. They can choose whether to take part in the research or not, and decide what views and experiences they will – or will not – share with the researchers.

3 *Influencing the decision making.* Young people can become more fully involved as young researchers; helping to influence how the research is conducted by offering their opinions on the research design and analysis, informing the workers' decisions (see Case study 7).

4 *Deciding partners.* Young researchers can work in partnership with workers, making joint decisions. The young researchers may be part of a team which includes adult researchers, and in some instances an adult research manager may have ultimate authority (see Case study 8).

5 *Main deciders.* Young people have the authority to make final decisions. They are usually supported by workers to help them make choices (see Case studies 9 and 10).

Case study 7 Youth transitions

A research project on youth transitions was decided upon by workers and research funders. A small reference group of young advisers was set up to discuss the work throughout the project. They helped to amend the research aims and to refine the methodology. The draft interview schedule was also piloted on them. The adult researcher conducted interviews with young respondents and discussed the findings with the reference group. The young advisers will have the opportunity to input at the analysis stage of the research and the dissemination of the findings (Save the Children research, in progress).

Case study 8 Further education for students with disabilities

Research carried out by Barnardos on further education for disabled students had a team comprising a research manager (who arranged access), an experienced research officer (who led the interview team) and three young research assistants who had recently left a special school. The research assistants were involved in all stages of the research design, were trained in interviewing techniques, and they co-authored the final report (Ash *et al.*, 1996).

In some projects, the young people have a large controlling role in many stages of the research whereas, in others, their influence is only limited to certain stages of the process.

Case study 9 Main deciders in all stages of the process: feasibility study for a local youth newsletter

The older members of a youth group had already been involved in carrying out research, and the younger members of the group (aged 14 to 16) also wanted to learn about research and carry out their own study. They were trained by both the older group members and a worker, and then undertook a small-scale needs assessment for a local magazine. They initiated the study and had full control over its design. The data they collected – although limited – were used in a successful funding application for a youth newsletter (YARD and Oldham, 1998a; for overseas example, see Okurut *et al.*, 1996).

> **Case study 10 Main deciders in some stages of the process:
> young people's mental health needs**
>
> Youth workers identified the need for research on mental health services
> from discussions with their young project users. They recruited a group of
> young project users who had used mental health services to undertake the
> research. The young researchers identified the most important issues to
> research. They received training in research and chose to use semi-
> structured interviews. They then designed the interview schedules and
> carried out the interviews. The young researchers also shared their own
> views and experience about mental health services with the adult
> researcher, to be incorporated into the final report. Workers transcribed the
> interviews, and the adult researcher analysed the data and wrote the
> research report. After the research process was finished, most of the young
> researchers had moved on to other things. The dissemination and
> development work following on from the research is planned to be carried
> out by other groups of young people (Laws *et al.*, 1999).

Assigning tasks

Decision making and action

A distinction needs to be made between (a) making decisions about
what has to be done, and (b) carrying out the tasks. The power
resides primarily with the first rather than the second of these. Even
where young researchers influence decisions or are main deciders
in a project, this does not mean that they have to undertake all the
tasks involved in the work. Instead, young researchers can
delegate or share the tasks with others, in the following ways.

- Workers carry out certain tasks, because of the young
  researchers' lack of time, interest, confidence or skills.

- Young researchers carry out tasks together with the workers –
  building on each other's skills and knowledge.

- Young researchers delegate tasks amongst themselves
  according to their own interests, skills and availability.

It is a good learning outcome for the researchers to appreciate that by delegating tasks they do not have to lose control; although they will need to be well briefed about the tasks in order to direct others.

Young researchers as respondents

The same young people can be involved in research as both research respondents and researchers, in the following ways.

- Adults research the views and experiences of young people, and then these young people collect the views of their peers for additional data (for examples, see Case studies 23 and 26 under 'Visualisation technique').

- The young researchers primarily collect the views and experiences of other young people (and/or adults), but they also include their own views and experiences about the issues being researched in the final report (for example, see Case study 10 earlier in this chapter).

Involving different groups of young people

Conducting research – from inception to dissemination – can take a long time. This may mean involving different young people at the various stages, rather than involving the same group all the way through, as illustrated in Case study 11 (see also Case study 10).

Case study 11 Participation rights in the North East of England

In a series of workshops run by Save the Children about children's participation in the North East of England, many children and young people said they wanted to put people in power in the hot seat. They wanted to ask them whether they listened to young people's views when making policies and decisions which affected their lives and, if not, why not. Save the Children therefore recruited another group of interested young people to do just this (Nevison, 1996).

Advisory and reference groups

Young researchers can be involved in research in an advisory capacity, impacting on the design and analysis of the research, in the following ways:

- join an adult-led research advisory (or steering) group

- have their own young 'reference' group in which they discuss the research.

Advisory group

Advisory groups made up of project workers, outsider professionals and young people have been found to be very useful within Save the Children (see section on 'Meetings with adults' in Chapter 3). In some projects, this group may also fulfil the role of a management steering group. These groups have several advantages:

- forum for discussing issues

- outsiders offer their informed views

- professionals help to identify other resources and support

- establishes a dialogue between professionals and young people

- encourages a wider ownership and commitment to the research findings.

If research is being conducted by adults, then having young people on the advisory/steering group may encourage other young respondents to participate in the study:

> I think that letting the respondents know that there were two school-age mothers already on the [steering] Group helped to encourage them to come along [to the group interview], they knew that they weren't on their own. (Young researcher, quoted in McDonald, 1996)

Reference group

A reference group is made up of young people from the community being researched who meet together to discuss the research and share their ideas with a research worker. This provides an opportunity for the workers to find out young people's ideas about the design of the project and to pilot the research tools (for example, Case study 7; also see Morris, 1998). This group will need to be recruited and supported in the same way as other groups of young researchers, as discussed in the next chapter.

The young advisers can also be research respondents; their views and experiences of the research subject can be collected and included in the final research report.

Use the form shown in Figure 1 to plan how the young people will participate in the research.

1   Indicate what level of involvement young people will have at each research stage.

2   Indicate who will carry out the required tasks at each stage.

Figure 1 Form to plan how young people will participate in the research

Stages in the research process	(1) Level of involvement • None • Be informed • Express a view • Influence decision • Partner decider • Main decider	(2) Who will carry out the tasks? • Young people • Workers • Partner agency
Commission/initiate research		
Set budgets		
Decide the research topic		
Set aims and objectives		
Recruit researchers/other workers		
Advisory/reference group		
Choose research methods		
Write research questions		
Collect information (fieldwork) • young people's data • professionals' data • community adults' data • secondary data		
Provide research data (i.e. own views/experience)		
Analysis		
Choose recommendations		
Write report		
Authorship		
Produce other product (e.g. video)		
Disseminate research findings		
Access to research findings		
Development and campaigning		

KEY LEARNING POINTS: How young researchers can participate

- Young people can take part in research in different ways, having varying degrees of control.

- There are many different stages in the research process in which young researchers can take part.

- It needs to be decided what level of involvement the young people will have at each of the different stages of research.

- Young people can be involved in research by simply being informed that research is being carried out by others, or by being asked to express their views as research respondents.

- Young people can be involved more fully as young researchers: by helping to influence the research design; by being equal partners with the adult workers, making joint decisions about the design of the research; or by being the main deciders about how the research should be carried out.

- Young researchers can be involved in helping to design research without necessarily having to undertake all the required tasks.

- Young people can be researchers – by designing and conducting research – and also be young respondents by including their own views about the subject they are investigating.

- Different groups of young people can be involved at different stages of the research process.

- Young people can be involved in research in an advisory capacity, by joining an adult-led advisory group or having their own 'reference' group.

$\mathcal{3}$ Setting up the project

In Save the Children's experience there are a number of important issues to consider when setting up a participatory research project with young researchers. These include being clear about which young people are to be involved in the project, the roles of workers and young researchers, and the type of support required, including how to maintain the interest and motivation of the young people.

Underlying all these decisions is the need to have good communication structures between all workers, partner agencies and participating young people, so that everyone has a shared understanding of the project process and expected outcomes. Where initial discussion does not take place, the work can end up being directed by an individual worker's own values and perspective. This may leave others – including the young people – feeling confused, with raised expectations and being disappointed by the project outcomes.

Recruiting young researchers

Defining the target group of young researchers

Deciding which group(s) of young people to involve as researchers will depend on the research topic and whether you already work with young people.

- *You have already decided the research topic.* If you want young peer researchers – who are representative of the population being researched – then sampling starts with their recruitment. You will need to decide how peers are defined, taking into account their similar experiences and status, as well as age; for example, young mothers aged 16 to 21, or Bangladeshi young people attending local schools. (For more information, see the 'Who are peers?' box opposite; and section on 'Should young people always research their own community?' in Chapter 1.)

- *You have not selected the research topic – or have chosen only a very broad area, such as 'health' or 'leisure' – and want to define it in consultation with the young people.* The target group of young researchers could be less tightly defined, such as 'local young people' or 'socially excluded young people'.

- *You work with an established youth group who wants to do some research.* Then your group of young researchers are already defined for you. You may still want to select from within this group; either because they need personal experience of the research topic, or because only some are able or want to take part in the project.

Who are peers? *Read on if you want to know more ...*

Deciding which young people are 'peers' or from the same 'community' as the target respondents can require some careful consideration. There are degrees to which someone is regarded as an insider or outsider by others in a community; people are defined as much by their differences as by their similarities. Naples (1997) argued that being an insider or outsider is not a specific social identity, but 'ever-shifting' – dependent on who you are talking to – and defined by class, gender, race and other dimensions of inequality. In her study of adults in two rural Iowa towns, she claimed never to have met 'a community resident who feels completely like the mythical community "insider"' because 'most felt feelings of alienation from the perceived wider community' (Naples, 1997, pp. 80–1).

It is therefore important to consider the young researchers' gender, ethnicity, relevant experience to the research topic, interests and the area they live – as well as, or sometimes instead of, their age. There may be some subtler social relations which structure relationships between young people – such as fashion and qualifications. Young people can also be territorial and may consider those living in other (even nearby) areas, those in another group or 'gang', or those attending another school, for example, as outsiders rather than peers.

Using older young researchers

Several research projects have involved older young researchers (in their mid to late teens and early twenties) to research younger respondents who are from the same community or who share similar experiences; for example, a care history of young Bangladeshis living in the same area (for examples, see: Fast Forward Positive Lifestyles Ltd, 1994; Hobbiss *et al.*, 1998b; Howarth, 1997). This can work well as the slightly older individuals can be more confident and can develop more advanced research skills.

There may still be times when young respondents are scared of older young researchers – as shown in Case study 12 – and every caution should be taken to ensure this does not happen.

Young researchers will need practice talking to others the same age as their intended respondents, and it should not be assumed that they will always 'relate' to those who are younger, or will have shared experiences. As Case studies 13 and 14 demonstrate, young researchers can use different language even to respondents only a few years younger.

Case study 12 Children's stay in hospital

A teacher in one study volunteered a group of girls (aged ten to 12) to be interviewed about their stay in hospital, and they were 'upset' by and 'scared' of the slightly older young researchers (aged 15 to 17) (Alderson, 1995).

Case study 13 Play and leisure needs of Bangladeshi children in Camden

Young researchers aged 15 to 18 interviewed others aged eight to 12 about their play and leisure needs. All the young people were from the local Bangladeshi community in north London. The young researchers had designed the interview schedule, but, when this was piloted with a group of 12 year olds, there were still many things the young respondents did not understand. The older researchers found it easy to talk to the younger respondents, and they had a shared knowledge of the local area which helped them to understand the children's accounts. They also found that the children continued to experience the same issues of racism, although they did have more play options than the young researchers had done only a few years before (Howarth, 1997).

Case study 14 Children's stay in hospital

The young researchers in Alderson's (1995) study were 15 to 17 years old and they interviewed ten to 12 year olds and some 15 to 16 year olds. The adults had believed they would find it easier to interview the youngest respondents, but the young researchers said it was easier to interview those their own age. They said they would have liked practice talking to ten to 12 year olds as part of their training, rather than practising just with the others their own age. One young researcher described the difficulties of interviewing those who are younger: 'You use different words – "confidentiality" doesn't mean much to a ten year old' (Alderson, 1995, p. 107).

What skill levels do the young researchers need to have?

Young people can become highly competent researchers with time and practice; developing a range of skills required to research their communities, including designing research tools and interviewing.

Research requires certain skills, although the many tasks involved demand different levels of knowledge and skills, as do various research methods (⊃ see Learning Resource Materials). It is important to balance the project demands with the capacities of the young researchers involved. Care must be taken not to over-estimate the young people's skills and abilities; having raised expectations and then setting them up to fail. At the same time, it is important not to under-estimate their skills and abilities; depriving them of the opportunity to fully take part and excel.

When designing the project, ensure one of the following:

* the recruited researchers have the knowledge and skills required to carry out pre-decided tasks, or

* the recruited researchers can be trained and supported to acquire the required knowledge and skills within the given time and resources, also developing the young people's basic abilities where necessary, or

- the design of the project is tailored to meet the different capacities and interests of the recruited researchers (including the less able and confident, and those with high support needs) (see section on 'Support', later in this chapter).

Recruiting a new group of young researchers

When deciding whether to recruit a new group of young people to undertake research, or to work with an already established youth group, consider the following.

- Recruiting a new group can take a long time, up to several months.

- More work is needed to build and maintain group cohesion within a new group.

- Workers may impose their own agenda on to the community if recruiting a new group, rather than responding to young people's own agenda.

- Recruiting a new group allows workers to select the most appropriate young people to do a defined research project; by identifying peers and those with the required skills.

- Established youth groups are more likely to remain together after the research is finished, and are therefore better placed to follow on the research dissemination and development work.

- If new groups are set up within existing organisations and institutions (including schools, residential homes, youth agencies, leisure centres, etc.) they will be better placed to continue working together after the research is finished.

Young people often have many competing commitments – including education, work, family, religious and cultural responsibilities, busy social lives, as well as other life issues which demand time and energy (such as health issues, dependants, living independently, claiming benefits, etc.). You may choose to work with disadvantaged young people, some of whom may have fairly chaotic lives – including drug and alcohol use, crime, imprisonment, homelessness, and mental health problems. These can all impact on their availability to take part in the research process, their reliability and whether they will stay involved throughout different stages of the process. Young people often drop out, so it is advisable initially to recruit slightly more group members or plan for new take-up later on.

Some projects use interviews when recruiting young researchers; particularly, if they are to be paid, if there are more people interested in the project than can be supported, or to ensure the young people have the required skills and knowledge. If you work with an existing group, other young people can also be encouraged to join the project. Issues to consider in their recruitment are outlined below.

- *Recruitment literature.* Ask young people to look over the recruitment literature – including leaflets and job descriptions – to ensure the language is 'young person friendly'.

- *Recruitment ground rules.* Ensure recruitment ground rules are established, including the following: equal opportunities, confidentiality, health and safety, child protection. Decide whether parental/guardian consent is required for those under 18 years old.

- *Outreach.* Visit youth groups, schools and other agencies. Also talk to young people wherever else they hang out – including the streets and shops – to access those who are not in touch with services. Leaflets and posters can be placed in all these places, and distributed using the local paper delivery system. The more time spent on outreach, the more likely it is that the final group will be representative of the target population.

- *Meetings.* Have meetings with interested young people; in groups or one to one. This enables them to find out more about the project and to get to know the workers.

- *Job description and person specification.* Draw up clear selection criteria before recruiting a group, listing what relevant knowledge or experience you want them to have. Take account of the fact that some applicants – particularly the younger ones – will have less experience and may be less confident. Include a task list in the job description.

- *Interviews.* If interviews are used, the interview panel will ideally include other young people who have been trained in selection procedures. Whilst the interviews might follow formal procedures, attempt to keep them chatty and to put the interviewees at ease.

- *Induction.* Develop an induction process for all new young researchers, including those who are later recruited to join an established group.

Young people can be involved in the recruitment of new workers – such as adult researchers – to ensure they can effectively communicate with young people (for detailed example, see Berridge, 1995).

Paying young researchers

Several groups of young researchers in Save the Children have been paid to undertake research, whereas others have not. Where the project is about their participation in a democratic process, then workers have often decided not to pay them. If the work meets a professional agenda – rather than the young people's own – then often they are paid to do the job being asked of them.

Advantages to payment

- Recognises the young researchers' contribution.

- Young researchers feel valued.

- Professionals can take the young researchers more seriously.

- Increases motivation and interest in the project.

- Helps to ensure tasks are completed.

- Can bring the young researchers into an organisation's internal decision-making structures, and give them more influence in this way.

Disadvantages of payment

- Payment can be a form of control; dictating how young people are to 'participate' rather than supporting them to work to their own agenda.

- Payment changes the relationship between the adults and young people. The workers become managers and direct what the young researchers do.

- If young people volunteer, they can 'vote with their feet' and participate only when they want to. This makes workers more accountable to the young people.

- Some young researchers may participate in the project for the money, and not because they are interested in the work.

- Paying the young researchers can set a precedent whereby they will want to be paid for any similar future work, which may not be sustainable.

- Payment can prohibit the inclusion of those under 16 years old, as there are complex regulations for the employment of this age group (see Pettitt, 1998; or contact your Local Education Authority).

- Payment can interfere with some young people's social security benefits, and they may need advice about this.

If you intend to employ young people – particularly those on benefits – it is worth considering offering longer-term contracts, with a sufficient number of weekly hours to make it financially worth their while. There are also other methods of reimbursing young researchers for their time and effort, including giving voluntary expenses, making a bulk payment to an established group or organisation to which the young people belong, and through residentials and social events.

Paying research respondents

The National Children's Bureau (1993) recommends giving respondents compensation for their time and trouble. Rather than offering this as an 'enticement' to take part, they suggest giving it at the end of their participation (e.g. at the end of an interview). Some projects do offer potential interviewees compensation before they are interviewed, as they feel the young people should not be expected to give up their time voluntarily.

Compensation is usually given in the form of vouchers (e.g. cinema, CDs, fast food outlets), rather than cash. It is worth checking with the young researchers to see what might appeal to their peers; rather than making assumptions about what they would like. Child care and travel should at least be paid.

Roles of young researchers and workers

Young researchers' role

Clarification is needed on what role young people have in relation to the workers, and this will be affected by whether they are paid or volunteer (see above section on 'Paying young researchers'). Their role has been defined differently on various projects, including:

* project users/volunteers

* partners/colleagues

* trainees/employees.

The choice of role has implications for how workers relate to the young researchers, which decisions they can make, and what responsibilities they can be expected to fulfil.

Workers' roles

Projects involving young researchers require both research and youth work support. Sometimes other specialist support is provided to meet the specific needs of a research group. Workers support the young researchers to undertake their own decisions and tasks, but adults may also carry out the more difficult, or boring, tasks.

Within Save the Children, two different workers usually undertake the research and youth work roles – as described below. In practice, the adult researcher and youth worker roles overlap (for more information see the 'The adult researcher's role' box). One worker can undertake both if she/he can dedicate the required hours, and has the necessary youth work and research skills, although it can prove difficult delivering all the necessary support alone and two workers are recommended. Sometimes a youth worker takes a lead in supporting the group throughout the project, and research support is provided intermittently by an outside consultant.

* Research support – to help the group learn about research; to explore how to design the project, to carry out any required fieldwork, and to help analyse and write up the findings.

The adult researcher's role: *Read on if you want to know more …*

Traditionally, a researcher is expected to interact in an (apparently) detached and impartial way, while a youth worker's role is more typically about the education and development of young people. Participatory research demands a combination of these roles – what Hart (1992, p. 19) described as the 're-professionalization' of the researcher's role into a 'democratic participant'. Here, workers provide the necessary technical support for the young researchers to carry out the tasks themselves, and they educate the young people by sharing knowledge and facilitating critical awareness, rather than imposing views and ideology (see section on 'Will there be added benefits to involving young researchers?' in Chapter 1).

[A] very important role for the researcher, is to use whatever knowledge or insights she may have of the larger causes influencing the problem, and to engage in a democratic dialogue with the participants over these larger causes. Through the process of carrying out this participatory research the participants not only transform some conditions related to a practical problem in their lives, but they also educate themselves about their general situation, thereby empowering themselves more generally for future action. (Hart, 1992, p. 19)

- Youth work support – to help build group cohesion and develop closer relationships with the individual young people. This includes supporting them to go out into the community to conduct the research and to deal with any personal issues.

Workers' intervention

All projects are constrained by a number of legal, organisational, professional and personal parameters. Workers need to address how to maximise the young people's choices within these restrictions.

Workers may occasionally find they have to override or renegotiate decisions made by the young researchers, either to maintain research standards and good practice, or to ensure the project goals are achievable (for examples, see section on 'The ethics of involving young researchers' in Chapter 6).

Workers can usually negotiate joint decisions with the young researchers – building upon everyone's knowledge and experience – rather than simply imposing their own views (for examples, see section on 'Designing the research tools' in Chapter 4). If the young people are deciding partners, then a consensus will be required by all those involved. Within Save the Children, workers will not let a group do something they do not agree with if the organisation will ultimately be held responsible for that decision.

When workers use their status to intervene, this calls for some personal reflection about why they are doing so, and an awareness of their own positions and interests. Those with expertise and years of experience can find it hard to let go of their power and enable young people to make their own decisions. Workers also have considerable power to manipulate a group to come up with the decision they want, in the following ways:

- workers continue group discussions until the 'correct' choice has been made

- workers' non-verbal behaviour signals what they think

- workers present limited information which affects the young researchers' ability to make informed decisions

- young people often follow suggestions made by experienced workers.

Clearly communicating what powers the workers have to intervene will ensure the young researchers are not left to discover their ideas count for less than they had imagined. Also, be careful not to encourage young researchers to think they can contribute to decisions that have, in reality, already been made by workers or partner agencies.

Working with partner agencies

If work is to be carried out in partnership with other agencies and established youth groups, this has implications about the roles of the different stakeholders and the ownership of research, which will need to be negotiated.

There can be conflicts between partner agencies about how to work with the young researchers, including how much responsibility they should have (see Hobbiss *et al.*, 1998a). If the partner agency has not done this type of participatory work with young people before, then it can be worth discussing the project process and required outputs in some detail.

Partner agencies and others that you may come into contact with – including gatekeepers to young respondents – will sometimes have different agendas, as illustrated by Case studies 15 and 16. It is

Case study 15 Young people's experience of care

On one project, the young researchers were to conduct interviews with young people about local authority care. They had arranged for a local authority worker to be in the next room, in case the respondents became upset. During the first interview, the worker listened to the conversation through the door, then entered and challenged the young researcher about asking leading questions, and demanded to listen to the taped interview.

Case study 16 Youth provision needs assessment

In an overseas needs assessment of local youth provision, the workers from a local partner agency observed the research training for their own learning purposes. It became clear that the workers doubted the capacities of the young researchers and were threatened by the bottom-up approach of the project, and they frequently voiced their own opinions during group discussions. The research trainer eventually suggested that all the workers, including himself, leave the room during certain group exercises to enable the young researchers to discuss their ideas without interruption or criticism.

advisable to formally agree the roles of all the workers involved, particularly those providing a supportive role to young people, to avoid potential conflict.

Support

Workers need to provide considerable youth work support on participatory research projects. The levels of support will depend on the group's needs and how much they are participating in the research. Young people often welcome high degrees of worker support and guidance – particularly if they are new to research – although there is a fine line between being unsupportive and over-involved. A balance is needed between allowing the young people free reign to make their own decisions and conduct the research in their own way, while giving them enough support and not burdening them with too much work and decisions to make.

> At the end of the day the choice was ours but we did get pushed or helped from the people working with us, including the steering group. (Young researcher, quoted in Kirby and Pettitt, 1998)

A range of support can be considered – for individuals and the group as a whole – and identified in negotiation with the group members, using an initial needs assessment and ongoing discussion. This way, the training and research tasks can be designed to match the needs and capacities of the individuals within the group, which helps to ensure the young people are not set up to fail and do not drop out. Appropriate support will also help the young people's own personal development (ↄ see Learning Resource Materials).

Workers can also inform the young researchers what skills, time and resources they can – and cannot – offer the group.

Conducting a learning needs assessment

The list below suggests the types of information that are commonly assessed for the different individuals within a group, using one to one or group discussions, observation and sometimes a short questionnaire (⊃ see Learning Resource Materials):

- relevant experience

- previous learning experiences (including school)

- knowledge of the community/research topic

- knowledge and experience of doing research (e.g. studied research or been a research respondent)

- skills and abilities

- capacity to learn new relevant skills

- commitment to the project

- interests

- availability (inform them of any minimum time commitments required)

- travel requirements

- dependants or other responsibilities

- perceptions of research and the project

- expectations

- health and other support needs (e.g. drug use, child care, pregnancy, housing status).

Group support

Being part of a group and making new friends is often important for the young people joining research projects. Workers can therefore help them to build the group identity and to make friendships, by introducing fun activities and group exercises, and by having social events throughout the project.

The participation of all group members can be supported using a variety of methods, including the following.

- Establish ground rules which outline what is expected from the young researchers and the workers.

- Encourage all the young researchers to voice their knowledge and experience of the issues being researched, and to contribute to the design of the research process.

- Encourage respect for every individual's contribution.

- Agree in advance how to deal with disagreements. When these occur, encourage an understanding of people's different views, and resolve conflict by democratic negotiation.

- Encourage those who tend to dominate within the group to take a back seat role – by asking them to take notes of discussions or operate a video camera, for example – or make use of smaller group and pair work.

The size of the group will have an impact on the research. Larger groups can make the training more fun, and they allow for more exercises, games and lively discussions. Smaller groups are better for more intense work, and one to one support. If some members of the group have high support needs, these may be missed in a large group.

Individual support

Their own personal development is frequently high on the young researchers' agenda. One to one support helps to ensure their experience of participating in the project is a good one, in the ways listed below. This support can be provided during supervisions or more informally.

- Set individual goals to allow for their own interests and capacities.

- Discuss concerns or ideas.

- Check understanding and progress.

- Offer support to deal with other events in their lives.

- Towards the end of the project, identify future opportunities in education, employment or community work.

If individuals – or the group – want to leave the research project, they should be supported to move on, and not made to feel guilty or pressured to stay.

Training

The young researchers will need training to undertake the required research tasks. Groups will not necessarily have to be trained in all research issues, but only those that are relevant to the tasks they are undertaking. The section on 'Maintaining motivation and interest' later in this chapter examines ways in which to ensure the training is made as interesting and relevant to the young researchers as possible (⊃ see Learning Resource Materials).

Research projects provide a good opportunity for the young researchers to develop transferable knowledge and skills, as well as learning about research. For example, interviewing helps to develop listening skills and quantitative data analysis can be taught using spreadsheets.

The young researchers may also require training on issues related to the research which will enhance their knowledge and skills; for example, presentation and media skills, and information on local services and relevant policy issues.

Formal recognition

Young researchers value receiving recognition for the work they have done, including the knowledge and skills they have learned. Examples include (⊃ see Learning Resource Materials):

- formal accreditation

- certificate of achievement

- portfolio of work

- being named in the final research report

- job reference.

In school or college courses which include a research component, the students can be supported to conduct projects which will also be of use to their communities, as illustrated in Case study 17.

Peer support

The young researchers often offer each other valuable support, as follows.

Case study 17 Participation rights in the North East of England

One group of sixth-form students conducted a research project as part of a health and social work course which included a research module. They interviewed policy makers to examine the extent to which children and young people are consulted by them. The group was supported by an adult researcher over one academic year (Nevison, 1996).

- *Peer support within the group.* This is particularly useful during the fieldwork stage, as they can share achievements, discuss solutions to problems, offload 'sad' or 'traumatic' events that have been disclosed by the research respondents, and allow individuals to take a break whilst others cover for them (see section on 'Disclosure of sensitive information' in Chapter 6).

- *Working in pairs or groups.* Young researchers are often encouraged to work in pairs, or small groups, to provide support. This can also be used to ensure a gender balance, and to keep those with stronger personalities and abilities equally distributed (see section on 'Young people's safety' in Chapter 6).

- *Meeting other groups of young researchers.* Linking with other generic youth groups and/or young researchers elsewhere enables groups to share ideas.

- *Include experienced young researchers in a new group.* One or two experienced young researchers can be recruited to a new group, to share their experience and help translate workers' jargon. Workers need to be careful not to ask those with experience to undertake more of the tasks.

- *Experienced young researchers help workers to train another group.* They usually need to develop their training skills and receive considerable worker support to do so.

- *Young researchers within the group offer training.* Those with relevant personal knowledge or experience can be encouraged to run training sessions for the rest of their group. For example, a deaf young researcher provided deaf awareness training to the rest of the young researchers, all of whom had different disabilities.

Meetings with adults

There are a number of ways in which the workers can support

young people who attend meetings which adults also attend, such as advisory/steering group meetings.

* Explain the role of the meeting/group to the young people.

* Initial confidence building to ensure the young people believe their role is valued in the meeting/group.

* Ongoing reassurance that the young people's role is valued.

* Avoid using technical jargon.

* Do not talk down to the young people.

* Do not exclude the young people; ensure you ask their opinions.

* Where literacy levels are low, use other media to explain and record decisions (e.g. tape, abridged minutes with simple clear language).

* Provide support between meetings to discuss further the young people's views, go over minutes and papers, check responses, monitor their feelings of involvement.

* Enable two or more young researchers to join the meeting/ group, to offer each other support.

* Address individual support needs as they arise.

* Be aware of the power to manipulate decisions.

* Ensure young people believe their views are considered important.

* Workers are open to listening to the young people and having them challenge their own assumptions.

* Ensure partner agencies are committed to participatory ways of working, which may need initial discussion and training.

* Workers can attempt to get to know the young people, and can do so by having joint social events.

- If preferred, the young people can have their own sub-group meetings, and feed in their views to the main group via a worker:

  Young researcher I: All of them were helpful and they didn't treat us as kids. They had to meet us on the same level, individual persons ...

  Young researcher II: The first time we called the steering group and we were on it I thought I would just be an additional person within there, not saying anything, but it was good. (Quoted in Kirby and Pettitt, 1998)

Maintaining motivation and interest

Research can be a dry, academic subject, and young people have often complained of being bored when learning about research or doing some of the more mundane tasks involved. It is therefore necessary to think of how to involve young people in ways that will maintain their interest and motivation. Inevitably, the young researchers will be less into some elements of the research process – as will the adults – and they will sometimes have to work quite hard. The emphasis should be on trying to make it as enjoyable as possible, however, for all those involved. How to do this will depend on the age, interests and abilities of the group you are working with, and should be decided in discussion with them. Some ideas are given below.

- An initial assessment and ongoing reviews are undertaken to ensure the project is designed to meet the needs of the individuals of the group; including their interests, knowledge and skill levels (see section on 'Support' earlier in this chapter).

- The tasks demanded are appropriate for the age and capacities of those involved, and will not cause undue stress or feelings of failure.

- The project timetable is not too long, but allows sufficient time to meet the group's needs. The group meets reguarly, without long gaps in between each meeting.

- Simple language is used, and technical jargon is kept to a minimum. Workers can fall into the trap of using technical language to (re-)establish their control (Martin, 1996).

- The training uses examples which utilise the group's own interests and experiences.

- The emphasis is on experiential learning; maximum time is spent on practical tasks rather than classroom learning. Young people most enjoy *doing* the research – particularly the fieldwork – rather than *talking* about it.

    I enjoyed this bit most; talking to people, meeting them … hearing their stories. (Young researcher, quoted in Kirby and Pettitt, 1998)

- Attention spans can be short, so keep sessions quick moving, active and short. Allow for adequate breaks, and interspace sessions with youth work games and a variety of tasks.

- The young researchers input and help to organise the training sessions.

- The young people choose which parts of the research process they each want to be involved in, and they are not required to undertake all tasks.

- The researchers receive incentives; such as social events, food, payment, etc. The social element of the group work is very important to all involved.

- Residentials are useful for getting young people away from their own environment – including other commitments and distractions – to get to know each other and have fun.

- The young researchers' other commitments and life issues are accommodated for, and the young people are supported through these where necessary.

- Young researchers are frequently committed to doing research because they want to help their community. Their motivation will be enhanced if research is about a personal issue or their own community, and they recognise there is a need for the research (rather than being told there is). (See section on 'Setting aims and objectives' in Chapter 4.)

- There are realistic potentials for change to services/policies – even small change is a great motivator and increases people's sense of achievement.

- There is the potential for the group to carry on working together after the research has finished. (See section on 'Future development work with young researchers' in Chapter 7).

Equality issues

(⊃ See Learning Resource Materials for how to introduce equality issues to the young researchers.)

Gender issues

When carrying out research, there are a number of gender issues to consider, as follows (see Dent, 1996; Hill, 1997).

- *Availability.* When are girls and young women available to join in?

- *Child care.* Can this support be provided, or reimbursement given, where necessary?

- *Location.* Where can young women safely meet and travel to?

- *Topics.* Does the research address topics relevant to girls and young women?

- *Voice.* Do the young women have an equal voice in the research meetings; could other methods be developed to ensure they do, including separate gender pair and group work?

- *Marginalised young women.* What attempts are made to include the young women who are hard to access, including young mothers, those with disabilities, and those from minority ethnic groups?

- *Matched interview.* Consider whether young women should be interviewed by young female researchers.

Ethnicity and cultural issues

There are a number of ethnicity and cultural issues to consider (see Hill, 1997), as follows.

- *Involvement.* What attempts are made to involve young people from different minority ethnic groups?

- *Commitment.* Allow for their involvement in different cultural and religious festivals and commitments.

- *Parental involvement.* Be sensitive to the role of the family in different communities.

- *Focus.* Rather than just examining communities as 'problems', consider the structural and institutional causes of these problems.

- *Cultural awareness.* Discuss different cultural perspectives, and consider whether the research questions address cultural issues and are sensitive to different cultural perspectives.

- *Language.* When researching those who speak another first language, the researchers should either speak that language or use an interpreter. Also consider translating the research findings to make them accessible to the community. The researchers may need some additional language support themselves.

- *Matched interview.* Where possible, match young researchers and research respondents from similar ethnic backgrounds.

Involving young people with disabilities or high support needs

Young people with physical or learning disabilities, or other high support needs, can be supported to participate in research (for further reading, see Beresford, 1997; Morris, 1998; Ward, 1997).

When working with young people with disabilities or high support needs, consider the following.

- Assess the individual abilities and support needs.

- Ensure adequate worker time to meet the individual support needs.

- Additional time is needed to ensure people's understanding of issues and concepts, including the time to repeatedly go over these.

- Check individuals' understanding.

- Provide additional one to one support between group sessions to meet individuals' support needs.

- Ensure workers have the necessary skills and experience.

- Where young people have low literacy skills or are visually impaired, clear and simple handouts can be prepared, or notes from meetings read on to tape.

- Running disability awareness training: even when working with an all-disabled group where hierarchies of disability can develop.

- Do not 'take over' tasks which the group wants to do, and can do, for themselves (see Case study 18).

Working with a mixed-ability group can be difficult and time-consuming for workers. It is important to assess whether workers can meet very diverse needs within one group or whether there is a danger that those with higher support needs will be excluded, and set up to fail. This is particularly an issue when working with young people with learning disabilities. Consider how to fully involve everyone in the group sessions, and be careful not to design the project around the most able young people (or vice versa). Case study 19 demonstrates the need for adequate worker support in these cases.

Case study 18 Education provision for young people with disabilities

A group of young researchers (aged 18 to 26) with a range of physical and learning disabilities researched education provision for those with disabilities. The group was keen to undertake all the necessary tasks themselves, and felt that if workers offered to do things for them – such as write letters – this was because of their disability. They told workers that if they felt unable to do tasks they would ask for help, but otherwise they would like to do everything themselves and to learn the new skills (Educable Group, forthcoming).

Case study 19 Disability support

Workers setting up a peer research project wanted to include a young researcher with disabilities. A seconded disability worker supported them to recruit a young man with a hearing disability, and he attended the first few group sessions to help induct the young man. After that, another young researcher became the young man's 'buddy' and supported him during the project. The group worked well together, but the project workers felt the disabled young man was not as involved in group sessions as they would have liked. With hindsight, they thought it would have been better to have the continued input of the experienced disability worker (M. Appleyard, 'SOVA Triumph and success young people research project', personal correspondence).

Working with different age groups

The age of the group you choose to work with will have implications for how you do the work. Deciding what age to work with will depend on the research topic, who is to be researched and the skills required (see section on 'Recruiting young researchers' earlier in this chapter).

Young researchers aged 14 – and younger – have been found to be capable of doing research, and similar training exercises have been used with this age group as with the older researchers. Their age may be related to the following, however:

* interests

* capacities

* support needs

* availability.

The younger age groups do tend to have shorter concentration spans and to require more fun activities and the use of simpler language. Those in their late teens or early twenties may be more able to grasp harder conceptual issues.

Mixed age groups (12 to 18 years) have been found to work well together, but it helps if the group members already know each other when there is insufficient time to develop group cohesion. The different interests and capacities within the group can be accommodated by designing and delegating tasks as appropriate.

Participatory budget setting

Professionals can use their financial influence to direct community development to their own agendas (Craig and Porter, 1997). As a result, young researchers rarely get access or control of budgets.

There is little reason why young researchers cannot, at the very least, be informed about the budget or even have a role in how all – or part – of it is spent, as illustrated in Case study 20. If young people are represented on an advisory or steering group, this provides a good opportunity to share budgetary information.

Involving young people in participatory needs assessments is another way of giving them a say in how agencies allocate budgets.

Case study 20 Young researchers' budgetary control

One group of young researchers was given control of £200 of the research budget, for their entertainment purposes; they could decide how and when to spend the money, including on what type of food they wanted on training days and their social nights out. This encouraged the young researchers to make joint decisions, and to take account of different dietary needs and social interests within the group.

KEY LEARNING POINTS: Setting up the project

- Good communication structures are needed between all those involved in the research, to ensure everyone has a shared understanding of the project.

- When recruiting a group of young researchers, careful thought is needed about which young people it is most appropriate to involve to research a particular issue.

- Young people need to develop skills to carry out research. Ensure that either the recruited young researchers have the capacities to develop the required skills and knowledge, or the project is designed to meet the young researchers' own capacities.

- There are a number of advantages to working with an established youth group, rather than having to recruit a new group of young researchers. For example, it saves time and can make the research more accountable to the community.

- There are a number of practice issues that need to be considered when recruiting a new group of young researchers; from designing appropriate recruitment literature to inductions.

Continued

- Young researchers are sometimes paid for their research work, depending on why they are involved and how much work they are expected to do. Research respondents are also sometimes reimbursed for their participation.

- The young researchers' role needs to be clearly defined, as this has implications for how they participate in the project. It is recommended that two workers – a youth worker and a researcher – support the group of young researchers.

- Research projects have a number of constraints, and sometimes workers may have to overrule decisions made by the young researchers. Workers need to be careful not to use their power to influence decisions unnecessarily.

- When working in partnership with other agencies, ensure the roles of each agency are fully negotiated and understood.

- Workers need to provide young researchers with a range of support, based on an ongoing assessment of their needs. This includes individual and group support, helping them to move on after the research, and enabling the young people to fully participate in meetings which adults also attend.

- Young people can find research boring, and therefore workers need to consider ways to make it fun, and to maintain the young researchers' motivation and interest.

- There are a number of equality issues that need to be addressed in research; including gender, ethnicity and culture, involving those with disabilities or high support needs, and working with those of different ages.

- Young researchers can, at the very least, be informed about the project budgets. They can also be involved in setting all or some of the budget.

4 Doing the research

This chapter explores how to involve young researchers in conducting research, from the planning stages to carrying out the field work. The research planning and designing stages can be lengthy, and the young people may need additional support to maintain their interest (see section on 'Maintaining motivation and interest' in Chapter 3).

Introducing research

The young researchers will have had varying exposure to research; at school, in the media, or as research respondents. It is therefore worth exploring what is meant by research with them, including the following questions (⊃ see Learning Resource Materials).

- What is social research and why do we do it?

- What are the different stages in a research project?

- What is the role of a researcher?

- What are respondents' rights? (see Chapter 6 on 'Ethics').

Setting aims and objectives

Sometimes, a research project's aims are pre-decided by workers; either before they apply for funding or before they involve young people in the project. Young people can also be involved in deciding the aims, in the following ways.

- Young people decide what issue they want to research, and then write their own aims and objectives (with the support of workers).

- Workers decide the research topic, and then write the aims and objectives in consultation with the young researchers.

- Workers decide the topic and write draft aims and objectives, but ask the young researchers to agree these and amend as they like.

  It was a big decision [to decide the aims and objectives] ... us making a decision which might affect the lives of [similar young people] everywhere, we felt responsible. (Young researcher, quoted in Kirby and Pettitt, 1998)

Adult-led research often focuses on children and young people as problems or examines their vulnerabilities. When young researchers select their own research themes, they can have other priorities. For example, two of the four young research teams within Save the Children who selected their own topic chose to examine sports and leisure provision for young people in their area.

Where workers do enable young people to develop their own research topic, they must be prepared to find that it does not fit in with their organisation's priorities. If this will be a problem, then be clear about the scope of research that workers will be prepared to support. The young researchers may also need help to select a topic that they will be able to explore given their capacities and the time available.

Young researchers will be more interested in subjects that have some personal relevance to them. For example, those from ethnic minority groups, or those who have been in care, often feel particularly committed to researching others with similar experiences, and are frequently driven by the desire to help their own communities.

Abstract conceptual research themes which might appear to be relevant to young people's lives – such as children's rights – are often not as interesting to them as are concrete subjects that have direct and immediate relevance to them, such as the quality of their services. This is particularly true for the younger age groups, as demonstrated in Case study 21.

Where the research agenda is determined by young people, this can be done in consultation with many young people rather than just the few young researchers, making the research more accountable to the wider community. The young people who decide what is to be researched do not have to be the same as those who carry out the research.

- Workers can identify the need to research an issue during their development work with a number of young people over a period of time (which could be a number of years).

- Workers and/or young researchers can consult different groups of young people about what should be researched.

- Workers can bring together one large group of young people to talk in depth about what should be researched in their area.

If young people are to write the aims and objectives, rather than just decide what topic to research, they will need some training on what is meant by these terms, and the differences between the two (⊃ see Learning Resource Materials).

If workers decide the aims and objectives, these will need to be explained and discussed with the young researchers. Working definitions of any key concepts or terms used – such as leisure,

Case study 21 Pupils' participation in school

In a project which looked at participation in school, a group of young people (aged 11 to 16) were keen to discuss and research what improvements could be made for the pupils within their school. They tended to focus on immediate practical problems – such as the conditions of the toilets – and the workers found it harder to encourage them to discuss what permanent structures could be set up within the school for pupils to influence decisions. (Save the Children and Whitley Abbey School, 1999).

community, health, poverty, participation – can help to ensure a shared understanding of what is being researched.

Exploring the research issues

A good introduction to the research can be for the young researchers to explore their own views and experiences about the chosen research topic. This allows them to find out their own standpoint and any biases that they may hold. It also helps to identify the key areas and issues to explore in the research study. In this way, the young researchers act as an initial focus group and, with consent, their views and experiences could also be used as data in the final report (see sections on 'Young researchers as respondents' in Chapter 2 and 'Confidentiality' in Chapter 6).

The young researchers can also be supported to find out more background information about their research project, including previous research, relevant information on their community, policy issues and how local authorities are structured. This will help to ensure they are better able to participate and carry out the research.

Choosing the research methods

The popular perception of social research is of one to one (structured) interviews or self-completion questionnaires, and most young people similarly hold this view. These methods are frequently reported in the media and young people have often experienced them as research respondents. Where young researchers are free to choose what research methods they want to use, they often want to use the quantitative methods that are most familiar to them; feeling more confident doing so, and recognising that these methods are widely accepted and respected (illustrated in Case study 22).

Case study 22 Young people's experience of leaving care

Workers discussed a range of traditional research methods – including various participatory approaches – with a group of young researchers examining young people's experience of leaving care. The group decided to use interviews, as they believed this would lend status to their research and it would therefore be taken seriously. They felt 'way out' participatory research methods – such as drawing and using diagrams – would not achieve this desired effect (Booth et al., 1998).

From a research perspective it is important to choose methods that will obtain the required research information and which the participating young people also feel comfortable using. If young researchers have a deciding role in choosing the research methods, it will be important to explore with them the advantages and disadvantages of a range of methods that might be used, helping them to choose methods which will be appropriate for their own project, taking into account what the research hopes to achieve. The different research methods can be presented in a number of ways (⊃ see Learning Resource Materials), as follows.

- Discuss a range of research methods with the group and then ask them to choose which is most appropriate.

- First, explore in depth what information is required for the research – including what questions need to be answered – and then discuss what methods could best be used to find this out.

- Use a range of research methods in the young researchers' own training to demonstrate how different methods elicit different types of information – as illustrated in Case study 23.

Using a range of different methods may help to utilise the different interests and skills within the research group, as illustrated in Case study 23 (for more information see 'Triangulation' box). This can also allow respondents to choose which method they want to participate in.

Case study 23 Pupils' participation in school

In an investigation on participation in a school (see Case study 4 for full case study), the workers used a range of research methods to get a group of young researchers (aged 11 to 16) to discuss their own views about the school – including group discussions, participatory visualisation methods (mapping, ranking, etc.), role plays and questionnaires.

The young research team reviewed the different methods used – including how much information they obtained and whether others would enjoy them – and then selected and designed their own research methods to use with their fellow pupils. Small groups of young researchers each chose to use different methods, reflecting their own interests, confidence and skills. Those interested in drama chose to use role plays, whilst others used questionnaires and an older group conducted focus group discussions (Save the Children and Whitley Abbey School, 1999).

Triangulation: *Read on if you want to know more ...*

Research conducted by young researchers can stand alone, or be used to complement adult research. Triangulation is the use of different research methods and/or multiple observers to help establish the validity of the data collected (see Macdonald and Tipton, 1993). If young researchers use different research methods, this introduces triangulation. Also, if both adult and young researchers examine the same research issue – both groups using either the same or different research methods – the triangulation helps to validate each other's data and cast different perspectives on the same research topic.

Participatory research methods

Participatory research methods – such as drawing and role plays – can be appropriate ways of researching children and young people. These attempt to replace the more formal forms of adult communication and enquiry – such as traditional interviews – with those that are more appropriate for younger people. They typically adapt the types of communication young people already use in ways that also generate research information. This helps young respondents to talk about and explain their experience and views, utilising their own capacities and interests, and makes the process more enjoyable. Examples of how participatory research methods have been used by young researchers are given in Case studies 24 to 26.

Boyden and Ennew (1998) have produced a useful training pack on using participatory research methods with children (also see Gosling and Edwards, 1995; Pretty *et al.*, 1995; Hill, 1997).

Case study 24 Written data

Content analysis

At *Children's Express*, children aged eight to 13 undertook a content analysis of how children are portrayed in the national press. They held a conference to publicise their research, which found, for example, that children are commonly stereotyped as 'victims', 'cute', 'evil' and 'brave little angels' (Neustatter, 1998).

Diary

A group of young researchers – aged 16 to 21– asked other young people who had been permanently excluded from school to complete a three-day diary about what they do during weekdays. Questions included, for example, how much school work they do, how much teacher support they receive and how else they spend their day. The diary was pre-printed and asked a number of set questions each day. Some of the young respondents were also given disposable cameras to photograph how they spent their time (YARD and Oldham, 1998b).

Internet

A London-based youth group gathered information about young people's access to the Internet and how they think the Internet can promote awareness about children's rights. The findings will be used to improve Save the Children's own youth site, 'Hot Savvy'. The group used questionnaires, and face to face interviews and group discussions. They also accessed young people over the Internet – via a facility (Internet Relay Chat) that facilitates live exchange – to discuss their views (Article 12 Richmond, 1999; see also Coomber, 1997).

Case study 25 Oral data

Poetry and drama

Children in a Ugandan primary school presented poems and drama to a leader about their concerns that local animals were using their pond. This resulted in children and adults working together to clean the pond and build a fence around it (Child to Child project in International Save the Children Alliance, 1997 (p. 427 *UN Convention on the Rights of the Children Training Kit*).

Case study 26 Visual data

Picture prompt

Groups of young researchers aged 12 to 16 helped to conduct an evaluation of the assistance provided by a Save the Children project between July 1996 and December 1997 in Tajikstan. The young researchers prepared drawings of the following scenes, to be used as a focus for the interviews:

- the village scene in the summer of 1996
- the Save the Children project's inputs to the village
- the hoped for impact on the village by December 1997.

These pictures helped to attract the interviewees' attention, and acted as cues to help the young researchers progress through the group interview. The young researchers needed practice using these cues and it was found to work better using one picture rather than a sequence of scenes. When used well it was considered an effective tool to aid discussion (Parry-Williams, 1998).

Picture questionnaire

Young researchers drew a picture of a Caribbean scene which included 34 issues to do with eco-tourism. They asked other young people to describe the scene, and ranked their environmental awareness – as low, average, above average or high – depending on how many eco-factors they recognised in the picture (Precht, 1998).

Photography

This method has been used as part of a consultation with children as young as three to eight years old. They were asked to show a new worker around their area, and were given cameras to take photographs of the things important to them. The children produced a report which included their photographs, drawings, maps and reports. Six of the children presented the report – complete with spelling mistakes – to councillors, and it had an impact as the new playground was replanned for inside the estate, rather than on the fringes, as originally intended (Miller, 1996; Save the Children, 1996).

Video

In one study, the workers felt that traditional surveys were insufficiently dynamic and innovative, and therefore employed a community arts worker to support the group of young people to say what life was like for them in their village. Together, they decided that video would be the best medium to use over the available three months. Their video – entitled *No Fun in Bilsthorpe* – included the following:

*   interviews with young people and adults in the community
*   a spoof film trailer about a local group of young 'gangsters'
*   a young women's group talking about how they started
*   young people's own views and comments about the village
*   an animation film about vandalism and crime (Miller, 1998).

Visualisation technique

A group of 15 year olds was involved as research respondents in an adult-led study of teenage sexual health. The group met regularly to discuss relevant issues, and was then trained in participatory research techniques. They designed their own visual research tool which they used to collect the views of other young people. They drew a picture of a health clinic on a large sheet of paper; they asked others to draw lines out from the building and to write or draw the questions they would have if going to a clinic (Sellers and Westerby, 1996).

Drawing competition

A group of young researchers held a competition asking others to design a local youth centre, which offered a top prize of £20, and all entrants entered a free draw for a prize of £25. Only 22 young people entered the competition, and, while a few had clearly made an effort, it was felt that some people had hurriedly sketched their ideas in order to enter the draw. The drawings offered some limited information on the type of activities young people frequently wanted to see in a local youth centre (Curley and YARD, 1998).

Designing the research tools

Young researchers are often involved in designing research tools – such as questionnaires, interview schedules, mapping and ranking exercises. There are different stages involved in designing research tools – listed below – all of which the young researchers can be involved in. Their participation at this stage is particularly beneficial (see Case studies 27 to 29) as they can think of subject areas to include that workers may not otherwise have thought of, help to choose appropriate language to use and devise innovative ways of asking the questions.

The stages in designing research tools are:

- decide the subject areas to include

- word draft questions

- design how to ask the questions (for example, visualisation method such as drawing or ranking, self-completion tick boxes, etc.)

- order of questions

- discuss the draft questions, order and methods

- pilot the research tool

- revise the questions, order and methods.

Case study 27 Young people's successful transitions to adult

The young researchers in one project had helped design a self-completion questionnaire, but the pilot found that young respondents still did not understand a number of questions. The young researchers worked with workers to revise the questions, and they thought of many ways to make the wording clearer: for example, they suggested 'worried' rather than 'apprehensive', 'labelled' not 'stereotyped', and 'a sense of right and wrong' instead of 'having morals' (M. Appleyard, 'SOVA Triumph and success young people research project', personal correspondence).

Case study 28 Young people's experience of care

One group designed a method of initiating a focus group discussion about leaving care. Informed by their own experiences of care, they wrote words and phrases on pieces of card (e.g. 'abandoned', 'needed my family', 'supported', etc.), and asked those in the discussion group to say which best explained how they remembered feeling when leaving care. The young researchers thought of more negative than positive words to describe their experiences – which is an interesting result in itself – so the worker encouraged them to come up with a more balanced list of phrases (McKeown et al., forthcoming).

Case study 29 Local young people's education, training and leisure needs

Young researchers were asking others what put them off using youth services, and they designed innovative ways of representing the factors which the interviewees were then asked to rank in order of importance (Curley and YARD, 1998).

For example:

MON£Y D I S T A N C E RACISM

A few groups of young researchers within Save the Children have designed research tools almost entirely alone whilst, in other groups, workers have played a large role in supporting them to do so. Sometimes, the workers take responsibility for the technical task of refining the wording of the questions and the research tool design, but they do so in consultation with the young researchers and based on the young people's initial ideas about what subject areas and questions to include. The workers' role is determined partly by what level of participation the young researchers have within the project (see section on 'Level of participation' in Chapter 2) and their skill levels. If young researchers are only minimally involved in the design of the research tools, this can reduce their feelings of ownership of the research (e.g. Saunders and Broad, 1997).

When young researchers are given the main deciding role in designing the research tools, they may sometimes write over-long questionnaires or interview schedules, or include leading or ambiguous questions. In these instances, workers may have problems deciding how much they should impose their own 'quality' standards (also see section on 'Researching children and young people' in Chapter 6). Sometimes they may choose not to intervene to get the young researchers to shorten or amend a questionnaire, whilst others may feel it is important to offer advice and technical skills, and to negotiate a mutually agreeable research tool. Some case study examples are illustrated in Case studies 30 to 33.

It can be worth asking experienced professionals in the relevant field (possibly those on the advisory group) for their advice and comments on the research tools.

Case study 30 Influencing the decision making

A young research team working on a health needs assessment had initially drafted a questionnaire but this had been taken away and reworded by workers, so much so that the young researchers felt 'cut off' from the questionnaire and they also thought some questions were poorly worded (Saunders and Broad, 1997).

Case study 31 Deciding partners I

In one project, the young research team brainstormed ideas for the interview questions, then the research trainer and one young researcher worked closely together to word and tidy up the interview schedule. All the young researchers offered their comments on the draft schedule and these comments were incorporated into the final version. This was felt to work well by the trainer as it built on her research skills and the young researchers' knowledge of the local community (Kirby and Pettitt, 1998).

Case study 32 Deciding partners II

In a research project looking at transitions to adulthood, the workers presented a list of 12 key words to do with transitions (for example, home, employment and survival), and the young researchers brainstormed ideas relevant to these themes. They then refined their list of ideas, rejecting duplicates and ambiguous terms, and from this list an adult researcher worded a draft self-completion questionnaire. The young researchers commented on the draft, which the workers then refined as a result (P. Roach, SOVA, personal correspondence).

Case study 33 Main deciders

In a study of food in residential care, the young researchers designed a very long questionnaire. The workers did not want to intervene to shorten the research tool as they wanted ownership to remain with the group:

Over 80 questions were developed – clearly too many for 'good' questionnaire design … we used a questionnaire which, had a final year undergraduate used in their dissertation, I would fail it. We interfered very little because we did not want the young people to lose ownership of what had been a creative process for them. (Hobbiss *et al.*, 1998a, pp. 5–6)

To design the research tools, there are a number of factors that will need to be explained and discussed with the young researchers. This should include what tends to encourage respondents to take part or not, and how different types of questions elicit different information (⊃ see Learning Resource Materials), as follows.

- *Different types of questions:* open, closed, leading, probes, checking, etc.

- *How to order the questions:* easy opening questions, sensitive questions later and non-sensitive closing questions.

- *Length and variety:* do not include too many questions, particularly in self-completion questionnaires, and vary the way questions are asked.

- *Good formatting:* clear design, attractive visuals, simple instructions.

- *Context:* research tools need to be adapted to the given context.

Young researchers can feel more confident about using fairly structured interviews or questionnaires, because this provides them with clear prompts for asking questions. Other methods can seem more daunting if they will have to remember what to do and ask. It is therefore important to develop research tools that are self-explanatory and to ensure the young researchers have sufficient practice to develop their confidence and skill in using them.

Conducting face to face research methods

Young researchers will require specific training and practice on how to undertake fieldwork that requires them to have face to face contact with respondents (⊃ see Learning Resource Materials). Issues to discuss and practise in the training include:

- introducing the research

- explaining confidentiality (see section on 'Disclosure of sensitive information' in Chapter 6)

- empathetic and non-judgemental listening

- recording the information (see section on 'Recording the data' later in this chapter)

- closing the session.

Many researchers – young or otherwise – find it difficult to be empathetic with those they are interviewing (for case study examples see section on 'The ethics of involving young researchers' in Chapter 6). It is therefore important to explore how to listen non-judgementally and to practise this skill (⊃ see Learning Resource Materials).

To build the young researchers' confidence and skill in carrying out the field research – and to help them to become familiar with the research tools – they often need plenty of support and practice, such as:

- role plays, and pilot interviews (with friends)

- discuss first attempts at interviewing, and explore how their questioning could have been improved

- video or tape practice interviews to discuss

- workers can demonstrate how to conduct an interview, using the young researchers as respondents

- the young researchers shadow an experienced researcher to conduct interviews, or show them videos of others conducting interviews, if possible.

> When I did the first interview I was a bit nervous but after a couple I was alright. Maybe I felt nervous because I didn't know what to expect. (Young researcher, quoted in Nevison, 1996)

Probing for more information – rather than prompting for specific answers – is an area of interviewing which inexperienced researchers (young and old) often find particularly difficult, and it is a skill that requires plenty of practice (➲ see Learning Resource Materials). Workers can demonstrate how the collected information will be analysed so the young researchers understand the need to

Example from an interview schedule used to examine the education support needs of young refugees (HAYS and Kirby, 1998)

'In what way are the schools in Britain different to those in your country?'

(Probe: teaching style, size of classes, discipline, hours of study, expectations, etc.)

probe for more information, and suggestions for probe questions can be included on the research tool.

Conducting group discussions

Some young researchers may find conducting group discussions with their peers more difficult than other methods as this requires a certain amount of confidence and particular skills – such as group management, facilitation and interpersonal communication.

> It was sometimes difficult for the researchers [aged 13 to 18] to handle their peers' outbursts or divergence from a question or task ... It was difficult for them to balance directing their peers on the activity with courteous behaviour. They required more experience and practice. (Precht, 1998, pp. 48–9)

Where young researchers are to use group discussions, additional time is often required to help them to develop their skills and confidence, again using plenty of role play practice (for discussion on group work with young people, see Hurley, 1998). Workers often run a focus group discussion with the young researchers as respondents – about the topic under investigation – to demonstrate how discussions can be facilitated. This also enables the young researchers to reflect upon their own attitudes and experience, it raises issues to explore in their research, and provides an opportunity for them to comment on and improve the questions being asked.

Young researchers may find it easier to run group discussions with people they know, although this is not always the case because friends can 'play up'. Sometimes, workers sit in on the group discussion – to offer support if needed – or they run it jointly with the young researchers, although some may feel this will inhibit the respondents.

Young respondents' enjoyment

As well as ensuring the young researchers have fun, it is important to maximise the young respondents' own enjoyment. Ways of doing so will depend on the age, abilities and interests of the young respondents, but might include the following (from Johnson, 1996, p. 33):

- short sessions

- range of activities

- breaks

- games

- group work

- if they are not enjoying the methods, stop and adapt them.

Face to face contact with adult respondents

If young researchers are to conduct face to face research with adults, they may feel more comfortable doing so in pairs or small groups (see section on 'Should young people research adults' views?' in Chapter 1). This provides them with moral support and helps to reduce the power imbalance between the adult and young people.

Sometimes it might be decided that young researchers will accompany adult researchers to interview adults – either to observe or to co-interview – so that the adult researcher can offer the following types of support (also see Case study 34):

- arrange access to professionals and other adults who the young researchers may not otherwise have met

- help to put the adults at ease, knowing they have a fellow adult/ professional present

Case study 34 Education support needs of young refugees

A group of refugee young researchers interviewed peers about their educational support needs. The workers and young researchers decided that it would be more appropriate for workers to interview the relevant education professionals and community adults for the research, as it was believed they would feel more comfortable talking to other adults. The young researchers helped to draw up the interview schedule for the professionals, and they accompanied the adult researcher to a couple of the interviews. This was felt to be successful as it gave the young researchers the opportunity to question the professionals, and it established a dialogue between the two, whilst also using the adult researcher's knowledge and confidence to probe deeply (HAYS and Kirby, 1998).

- use their 'insider' knowledge to help interpret professional jargon and probe further

- be responsible for taking detailed written notes

- provide the young researchers with the opportunity to observe an experienced researcher.

Recording the data

Consideration will need to be given to how the young researchers will record the collected information, and they will need practice using their chosen method.

Many young people – particularly those with low literacy skills or confidence – rarely enjoy the idea of writing many notes to record research data. A lack of confidence can influence young researchers to choose self-completion questionnaires so they do not have to write, but there are other ways in which they can record information with little or no writing.

Writing

If the group needs to make written notes, there are ways to make this easier (⊃ see Learning Resource Materials).

- If the researchers work in pairs or groups, then one can ask the questions while another records the information.

- Design the interview schedule so that it is easy for the young researchers to write their responses, for example, leaving spaces after each question, and providing tick boxes where possible and appropriate.

- Give the group guidance on how to take notes, including simple forms of shorthand.

- During group work, the young researcher can record the main information on a flip chart in front of the research respondents. The respondents can also be encouraged to write comments themselves.

- Diagramming and visualisation methods can be designed so that discussion points are written on the diagram, or the respondents draw and/or write their own responses.

If the young researchers find writing hard, this may slow up the face to face contact time, possibly making it boring for the respondents. In that case, it may be best to consider another method of recording the information.

Tape recording

Tape recording the information ensures all the data are collected – and the full depth of qualitative information retained. This helps to underline the young researchers' competence at gathering information – rather than stressing their lack of writing skills. The recordings also allow other researchers to listen to the data which can aid analysis. Using tapes, however, may inhibit the respondents and make them worry more about confidentiality, particularly if researching a sensitive issue.

If using a tape recorder, then encourage the young researchers to practise doing so first. This should include asking the interviewee if they can be taped and checking whether the tape is recording at the start of the interview. The young researchers may need support to remember to always take their tape recorders, tapes and spare batteries/mains leads to the interview.

The young researchers should try to listen to the tape as soon as possible after the interview, to ensure they can still remember what was said if the tape is unclear. The young researchers can make notes from the tape – using a blank interview schedule as a guide – or transcribe the full interview conversation. If someone else is to transcribe the interview, it can be useful for the young researcher (and respondent, where possible) to check it as well. Transcription is a lengthy process, and it can be expensive to pay others to do it.

Workers record information

Workers can accompany young researchers and record the necessary information – either by making their own written notes, or by writing what the young researchers tell them to record (for example, Parry-Williams, 1998). The worker's presence may inhibit the respondent, however.

Case study 35 Bangladeshi street children

In Bangladesh, a group of young researchers – who could not read and write – interviewed other street children. They asked only a few questions and then remembered the answers until they met with a worker later that same day. They verbally recounted the interviewees' answers, which the worker recorded (Khan, 1997).

Video

Video can be used to record the interviews to ensure the information is easy to review and analyse. Video also allows researchers who were not present to have full access to the data for analysis. There is still a question of how the information is to be analysed from the screen – full transcriptions or written notes can be made – both of which are time-consuming. It can also make the respondents more self-conscious and make the interview less naturalistic. Video may raise concerns about confidentiality, and respondents may not want to be videoed. In addition, this method is expensive and rather cumbersome.

Accessing respondents

The young researchers can be involved in deciding which groups of young people and/or adults are to be researched, and where they can be accessed. This should include a discussion on equality issues, to raise the group's awareness of involving different groups of people in the research. Complex sampling theory and jargon should be avoided (⊃ see Learning Resource Materials).

As discussed in an earlier chapter (see section on 'Will young researchers have better access to those being researched?' in Chapter 1), young researchers can have difficulties accessing young people beyond their own friendship networks. One group, for example, arranged an open day for local young people to attend, but only a few turned up. Negotiating access to others – either through professional agencies or by approaching young people they do not know – is often the part of the research process that young researchers least like doing; and is a stage where they can become frustrated and lose motivation and morale. The time needed to negotiate access can easily take up to a few weeks.

Young people will require support and practice to ensure they are confident about negotiating access via professionals and asking respondents – both adults and young people – if they want to participate in the research (⊃ see Learning Resource Materials). Workers can do some preliminary work by finding out what local agencies are available, making initial contact and even negotiating access in advance where time is limited.

Where access has been granted, the young researchers sometimes feel they are not respected and supported by the professionals in the way that adult researchers are (e.g. Alderson, 1995). Agency workers can have understandable concerns about the research – particularly if it is evaluating their services – and a large degree of sensitivity may be needed to gain their assistance. It is also good practice, and can help gain access, to explain to both adults and other young people why young researchers are doing the research, to enable them to make informed decisions about whether to participate.

If agencies refuse access, then the young researchers' peer networks may have to be retried; for example, to find friends of friends who go to a particular school, live in a residential care home, or those who have attended a particular hospital.

KEY LEARNING POINTS: Doing the research

- The young researchers will need support and training to develop the confidence and skills to design and conduct research. This can take a considerable amount of time.

- First, introduce what is meant by research and what is the role of the researcher.

- Young researchers can be involved in setting aims and objectives. Other young people in the community can also help select the research topic. Young people's choice of research subject may be different from what workers would like to prioritise.

- Inform the young researchers about relevant background issues to the research and explore their own views and experiences of the research topic.

- Young researchers can be involved in choosing what research methods to use. They often prefer to use quantitative research methods, which are familiar to them, and may need some encouragement to consider other methods. Using a range of methods can help to utilise the young researchers' different interests and capacities.

- Participatory research methods can be appropriate ways of researching other young people and children. They can be more fun for the young people to use, and build on their own methods of communication.

- Young researchers can be usefully involved in designing research tools, with training and support. They can think of areas to include, choose appropriate language and design innovative ways of asking questions. Workers will need to decide the extent to which they will impose their own quality standards, by undertaking the technical task of refining the research tools.

- Young researchers will need to be supported to carry out face to face methods of research, and be given plenty of opportunities to practise these skills, including: introducing the research, explaining confidentiality and non-judgemental listening.

- Some young researchers find it hard to conduct group discussions. They will need additional practice and workers can co-run discussions with them.

- It is important to ensure the research is enjoyable for young respondents.

- There are a number of ways in which the young researchers can record their research data. They will need practice using their chosen method(s).

- The young researchers can be involved in deciding where to access the respondents to be researched. They will need support and practice to develop their confidence to approach young people and adults. Finding enough respondents takes time.

- Young researchers will need support to conduct face to face research with adult respondents. The young researchers can interview adults together with workers.

5 Analysis and write up

Analysing data

This section is about how to involve young people in the analysis stage of the research process, and not about how to analyse data (for information on how to analyse data, see Denscombe, 1998; Hall and Hall, 1996). During the analysis stage of the research, researchers can exercise a considerable amount of control as they sort, select, interpret and represent the collected data. Young people are often excluded from this part of the research process, even if they have been involved in undertaking the field work.

Involving young researchers in the analysis of data can prove difficult as the methods for doing so are still in the early stages of development. Young researchers are frequently uninterested in becoming involved in the analysis process which is perceived as long, boring and hard. They are likely to need additional encouragement and plenty of support to take part.

Young researchers have been known within Save the Children to vote with their feet and opt out of the analysis, when workers had hoped they would become more involved. It should be acknowledged, therefore, that some young people will not want to be involved at this stage of the research process – or they may want to be involved only in a small way.

It is often decided – by workers and/or young researchers – that an adult researcher will carry out the analysis. It can be hard for workers to analyse data they have not collected themselves, as they lack the additional information that field researchers pick up through intonation, body language, context, etc. If a worker does the analysis, it can therefore be an advantage to do so in consultation with the young field researchers.

Where young researchers are involved in the data analysis they can:

- include their understanding of the data

- raise issues that the workers might otherwise have ignored

- help to develop a deeper understanding of the research findings, based on their own related experience and their understanding of the language used by respondents

- use their insider knowledge and shared experiences to pick out 'discrepancies between what the respondents expressed and what they knew to be commonly held views among their peers' (Precht, 1998, p. 37)

- know and understand the research findings; thereby maintaining a sense of ownership of the research process

- make the adult researchers accountable for their analysis of the young people's views.

Involving young researchers in the analysis of quantitative data is relatively easy if it just demands frequency counts, percentages and simple comparisons, although complex statistical analysis will require a statistician. Analysing qualitative data is a more complex process of categorising and theory building. Workers need to beware of involving young researchers in ways that simply turn rich data into frequency counts, and of selecting 'juicy' quotes, which give a superficial understanding of others' experiences.

One way to involve the young researchers is to ask them to read and comment on the adult researchers' analysis of the data. While some will willingly do this, others will feel too removed from the data, and even uninterested and bored by this process – particularly if it has been a long time since the fieldwork was undertaken, and if they are expected to read large amounts of text.

The young researchers can be involved in more meaningful ways, listed in Table 7 (⊃ see Learning Resource Materials). They can be involved in analysing all the data, or, more realistically for many groups, by examining just parts of it. The group can be divided into pairs or small groups, each of which undertakes a different task. This might mean, for example, that they each take a different part of the data to analyse, depending on what they are interested in or have specific insider knowledge about. The use of both qualitative and quantitative analysis software can make the task of analysis simpler and more enjoyable for the young researchers, but this will require additional training.

The young respondents can also be encouraged to take part in the analysis of their own data (see Table 8). This helps to ensure the findings reflect their views and experiences as accurately as possible, rather than relying only on the adult and young researchers' interpretation of their accounts.

Case study 36 Pupils' participation in school

In a school survey (see Case study 4 for full case study), more younger than older pupils were found to believe that the school dinner queues are too long. When the young researchers' group was asked why they thought this might be, they explained that older pupils often queue barge in front of the younger ones (Save the Children and Whitley Abbey School, 1999).

Table 7 Examples of how to involve young researchers in the data analysis

Element of data analysis	Examples of involvement
Comment on the research process	Complete a form after each fieldwork contact detailing what main issues were raised, how open they felt the respondents were, their views on what the respondents said, how the contact could have been improved, etc.
	Discuss the data with workers as soon after each contact as possible, explaining what was said, and adding comments that they were unable to record at the time.

Continued

Table 7 Examples of how to involve young researchers in the data analysis (continued)

Element of data analysis	Examples of involvement
	Discuss the data with the whole group; including their impressions of the respondents' views, how representative the views were, etc.
Code and categorise the data	Code quantitative data and put this on coding sheets (which need to be clearly and simply designed) and/or computer software.
	Brainstorm the initial list of 'categories' for qualitative data analysis.
	Code qualitative data from survey open questions (including 'other' options to closed questions), doing so question by question.
	Code qualitative data from field notes or transcripts, doing so a paragraph at a time.
Interpret the data	Undertake quantitative analysis, choosing which frequency counts and percentages to calculate.
	Examine the adults' analysis of the quantitative data – presented in tables – and write their own description of these.
	Suggest possible relationships and comparisons to investigate within the data.
	Discuss directions of influence between key variables, visualising them using diagrams and arrows.
	Discuss possible explanations for the findings.
	Check adult researchers' interpretation of the data, particularly where the data is ambiguous.
	Select which quotes to use to illustrate the findings.

Table 8 Examples of how to involve young respondents in the data analysis

Probe respondents to explain the meanings of what they have said, or to explain the picture they have drawn, the role plays they have performed, etc.

Have a debrief – at the end of the research session – and ask the respondents to say how they found taking part in the interview, what could have been improved, how freely they felt able to talk, etc.

Give respondents their interview transcripts, allowing them to add to, delete or correct the comments they have made.

Discuss the initial analysis of the findings with groups of young respondents who were involved in the study – as well as the young researchers.

Level of interpretation

A consideration for the participatory adult researcher is whether to simply accept young people's own analysis of their situation or to build in wider social and economic factors (see Trinder, 1996 for review). When workers further interpret data collected by young people, this calls for increased reflection about how and why you have arrived at your final analysis.

There is a potential tension between the young researchers' insider knowledge helping them to inform the research and the problem of being emotionally involved in the subject matter which may prevent some from distancing themselves from the material, as can be seen in Case study 37. It is therefore important for the young people to understand their role as researchers before analysing the data, and for them to discuss how to represent the views and experiences that they oppose (see section on 'Introducing research' in Chapter 4).

Note that the education young researchers gain through their involvement in research projects (see section on 'Workers' roles' in Chapter 3) can alter their interpretation of other young respondents' views – becoming more aligned with the workers' views – as illustrated in Case study 38.

Case study 37 Representing opposing views

A group of young researchers disagreed with the views of some of the respondents' negative assessment of professional support. They discussed whether to include these opposing views in the report and, although they decided they would, one young researcher refused to present these views at the launch of the research (Save the Children Staff Workshop, 1998).

Case study 38 Eco-tourism in Grenada

As part of a project which examined the impacts of tourism on the local environment in Grenada, young researchers were taught a lot about eco-tourism, and this impacted on their analysis of the data they collected.

There was a contradiction between what the [young] researchers had expected and what the respondents actually said about tourists. They attributed the difference to respondents' 'indoctrination' on tourism, which hadn't allowed them to think about both the positive and negative factors … Researchers noted that since the respondents hadn't had the kind of education they'd had on tourism during the project, the students might not really know what they think about the topic. (Precht, 1998, p. 49)

If the workers' and young people's interpretations of the data are different, these can be presented separately, as follows.

- Present the workers' interpretation with the young people's comments on these.

- Present the two interpretations separately (for example, on either side of the page or in different reports).

- Adult researchers can publish more theoretical papers as separate journal articles.

Choosing the recommendations

Young researchers can use their knowledge and experience of the research subject to devise workable recommendations which resolve the issues identified in the research findings. Even if the young researchers have not been involved in analysing the data, they can still be usefully involved in writing recommendations. This way, young people are integral to deciding what needs to be changed, rather than adults having to bring young people round to their own decisions (Parry-Williams, 1998).

It may be necessary to explain and discuss the ways in which recommendations can fulfil the following:

- relate to questions raised in the research findings

- reflect the views of all those consulted

- identify achievable outcomes, taking into account available resources

- identify structural causes of problems

- target a range of audiences – including young people, parents, local professionals, government, etc.

Writing the report

The type of report required will depend on who is the intended audience. Sometimes, different reports are produced for various audiences, such as a formal report and a summary of the key issues.

Often, the young researchers will not want to write reports because they do not have the required time, skills, confidence, or interest. If workers write the report, then the young researchers can read it and make comments, although many will not relish the prospect if the text is long and dull. If so, there are other ways in which the young researchers can be involved (⊃ see Learning Resource Materials), as follows.

- Read and comment on all/some sections of the workers' report.

- Write some sections of the report. For example, the introduction, methods section, recommendations, etc.

- Write about their personal experiences of the project, and what they got out of being involved.

- Write their own short account of the project, which is presented in a report alongside the workers' (and partner agencies') accounts (for example, see Connolly *et al.*, 1996).

- Help to design the structure and format of the report.

- Choose the design – colours, fonts, illustrations, etc. – of the cover and/or contents.

- Take photographs, draw cartoons or other illustrations.

- Decide the title for the report.

If young researchers write sections of the report, an editorial decision will be needed about the extent to which their contributions will be corrected for spelling and grammar, while maintaining the young people's dominant voice. This can be negotiated with the young people themselves.

Producing translations of the full report or summary findings may need to be considered when the report is about communities who have another first language. This can be time-consuming and expensive, but is an important part of participatory research which seeks to inform the community being researched.

Producing other products

The young researchers can maintain a greater sense of ownership of the research project by designing their own report or another product. This other product may also be a better way of disseminating the research findings to audiences that would not read the 'formal' report; including young people and other community members (⊃ see Learning Resource Materials). Examples include:

- smaller written report – such as a summary or magazine – and illustrated with photographs or other illustrations

- leaflet, poster

- postcard with main findings (useful to send to anyone you want to influence)

- video

- photography exhibition – illustrating the project and the topic researched

- Internet site – design a new site, or provide information about the project to put on another existing site.

Detailing the research process

As the involvement of young researchers is a relatively new area of development, reports can help to share practice by detailing how the research was done, how young people were involved and how well the process worked. This is something the young people can become actively involved in discussing and writing – adding their own comments or 'quotes' (see section on 'Evaluating the research' in Chapter 7).

Whose name should go on the report?

Whilst participatory research may go some way to empowering local people, John Stanfield (1998) pointed out that it is rarely the participants who gain the 'career rewards', such as co-authorship. There are some exceptions (e.g. Ash *et al.*, 1996), but even where the young researchers have done all or most of the research – except writing the final report – they are often excluded from authorship.

It is important to discuss whose names are going to be on the report (or other materials), and to ensure all young people involved are recognised for their contribution. It can help the reader if reports clearly indicate the degree to which the workers and young researchers participated in the different stages of the process; including who commissioned it, chose the aims, selected the methods, wrote the research questions, analysed the information and wrote different sections of the report (see Case study 39).

Case study 39 Whose name goes on the report?

1   In one Save the Children project, the worker had written the report for a piece of peer research and was the only named author. A young person in the group queried why the young researchers were not named as authors given that they had designed and conducted the research.

2   In another Save the Children project, where the worker had written the report and only the researchers' names were given as authors, this led others to think that the young people alone had written the report. The skills and knowledge of the group were therefore misrepresented and others expected them to explain what was in the text and write similar reports in the future.

KEY LEARNING POINTS: Analysis and write up

*   Young researchers are often excluded from analysing research data.

*   Young researchers are frequently uninterested in the analysis which is considered to be difficult and boring. They need additional worker support to be involved at this stage.

*   The young researchers' involvement in the analysis has a number of benefits. These include developing a deeper understanding of the data and making the research more accountable to the young people.

*   When young researchers are involved in the analysis, care must be taken not to just complicate data.

*   Young researchers rarely want to read long texts on the research findings. There are other ways in which they can be more meaningfully involved.

*   Young researchers can comment on the research process, and code and categorise data, as well as help to interpret the findings.

*   The young respondents can also be encouraged to comment on the research process and to help interpret their own data.

*   Workers need to decide whether to include only the young people's interpretation of the data or to build in wider social and economic factors. It may be necessary to discuss with the young researchers how views they oppose will be included.

*   If workers and the young researchers have different interpretations of the data, these can be presented separately.

*   Young researchers can help to produce workable recommendations.

Continued

- Young researchers will often not want to write long research reports, but they can contribute to the workers' report and/or produce their own report.

- Young researchers can also produce another product, such as a video or leaflet, to disseminate the research findings.

- Reports can help to share practice in this new area of research, by including details and comments about the research process.

- A decision needs to be made about whose name goes on the report. It is important to recognise the young researchers for their contribution to the project.

6 Ethics

There are a number of ethical issues in conducting research, and some which are specific to research involving children and young people. Some are to do with how to research children and young people, and others concern involving young people as researchers. Many of these issues need to be considered at the research planning stage, but others will be ongoing throughout the research process, and workers and young researchers will need to be continually reflective about the work they are doing. Thought needs to be given to how the research process will impact on both the young respondents and the young researchers, without being overly protective and thus reducing their opportunities to participate.

Researching children and young people

It is not possible to detail the ethical considerations of researching children and young people, within the confines of this publication. These considerations are explored by others elsewhere (for example, Mahon and Glendinning, 1996; Mauthner, 1997; Morrow and Richards, 1996). Alderson (1995) provides a useful overview and check-list of questions to consider when carrying out a piece of research with respondents who are children or young people, such as consent and possible impacts of the research. The issues these authors raise are important whether an adult or a young person conducts the research, and should be discussed with the young researchers, including respondents' various rights (⊃ see Learning Resource Materials).

The ethics of involving young researchers

There are a number of ethical issues which are specific to involving young people in designing and carrying out research. By participating in research, the young researchers fulfil their right to seek and impart information, as laid down in Article 13 of the UN Convention on the Rights of the Child. They may only exercise this right, however, if they do not thereby violate the rights of others. Ethical issues can arise when there is concern that an unskilled young researcher might impact negatively on the respondents, or collect unusable data, which would misrepresent or silence the voice of those being researched, denying their right to express an opinion.

The type of ethical questions that have arisen, and the range of solutions explored, are outlined below. It should be clear from the level of participation decided for each project about whether the young researchers or workers will ultimately decide how to resolve these issues (see sections on 'Level of participation' in Chapter 2 and 'Workers' intervention' in Chapter 3).

Inappropriate language

What do you do if young researchers want to include 'inappropriate' (e.g. abusive, sexist, etc.) or 'invalid' (e.g. leading, unclear, etc.) questions or interpretations in the analysis?

- Workers can attempt to negotiate with the young researchers to change the questions.

- The workers and young people can write the questions together – building on each other's skills and knowledge – although full negotiation can take considerable time.

- Provide background training on the issues relevant to the research so that the young researchers make informed decisions.

- Run equality training.

Research skills

If there is concern that young researchers lack the necessary skills after training to interview appropriately and sensitively, should they be allowed to interview others (also see Case study 40)?

- Workers have a responsibility to all the research respondents in the project, and need to monitor the impact of the research on all those involved, not just the young researchers.

- Who decides whether they are sufficiently skilled? This could be adults, young people, or the two together.

- Recruitment can be used to determine young researchers' skills and understanding.

- Further training and discussion can be used to develop their skills and understanding.

- A larger group of young people may be involved in overseeing the research and, from within this group, they can select who is most interested and capable of doing the face to face contact with others.

- If different research methods are used, then these can build on different people's capacities and give everyone a chance to be involved, each doing the tasks that meet their interests and capacities.

- Young researchers can go out in pairs or small groups which include young researchers with a mix of skills and abilities.

- Ultimately, if the worker still has concerns about the young researcher, they may have to prevent them from interviewing other children/young people, or accompany them to all their interviews.

Case study 40 The need for empathetic research skills

1   In one Save the Children project, the worker was concerned that a young researcher's attitude to interviewing was inappropriate as the young person saw it as a means of control and an opportunity to interrogate others. In this instance, the young person dropped out of the project before the fieldwork began.

2   In another project, the worker was concerned about the deep-rooted sexist views of one young researcher, which were expressed in his blatant language and comments. There was no time to run equality training, and therefore the worker talked to the young researcher alone, and explained her concerns. The young researcher was paired up with a young female researcher, and the worker accompanied them to all their interviews.

3   In a research project in Tajikstan, workers were particularly struck that the young researchers – aged 12 to 16 – did not automatically empathise with the children they interviewed. They needed clarification and discussion about their role as interviewers and role play exercises to adopt a more caring and sensitive approach to the interviews, otherwise it was thought they might do more harm than good. After the pilot stage, the young researchers were told the work was now to begin in earnest and that it was going to be hard; this was to provide them with 'ample excuse to leave' if they wanted (Parry-Williams, 1998, pp. 5–6, 76).

4   During a group activity in which respondents were asked to look at a picture of a Caribbean scene and describe the images, some did not respond much to the questions being asked. Workers noted that this frustrated the young researchers (aged 13 to 18) – 'leading to some impatience during interviews' – which they felt may have biased some of the answers (Precht, 1998, p. 51).

5   In one project, some of the young researchers made it clear to respondents – particularly those they knew – what they thought of their responses to questions. One young researcher exclaimed 'you can't say that!' when they disagreed with a respondent's answer. The workers felt that the young respondents were not as overwhelmed by the young researchers talking this way as they would have been by adults, however.

Consent

Young researchers do not always feel they should have to seek the consent of adults to speak to children or young people (for example, Alderson, 1995). Frequently, they do not attempt to get consent if they interview friends or snowball out to friends of friends, rather than accessing young people through adult gatekeepers.

- Discuss with the group the benefits and problems of getting the consent of adults to interview children/young people.

- If adult consent is not sought, then ensure the group understands the importance of getting informed consent from children and young respondents, and that others must not be made to feel 'bad' if they do not take part.

Research ethics committees

Ethics committees which review research proposals are common within medical research, and in psychological research, but far less so in social research. Such committees can prove useful by safeguarding the research subjects' interests and checking research methodology, but can also serve to protect professionals and institutions; promoting their agenda rather than the rights of the research respondents (see Alderson, 1995; Morrow and Richards, 1996), as shown in Case study 41. A decision will need to be made about whether to access respondents through routes that require ethics committee approval, or to use alternative avenues, including the young researchers' informal networks.

Case study 41 Young people's mental health needs

In one study where young researchers wanted to research the mental health needs of other young people, the health authority's ethics committee was very critical. They queried how those with a history of mental distress would know if what the interviewees were saying was true, and they demonstrated their bias towards quantitative research by recommending the need for a statistician. The young researchers conducted the study without the approval of the ethics committee (Save the Children Staff Workshop, 1998).

Disclosure of sensitive information

Coping with disclosure

Even when talking about the most apparently innocuous subjects, respondents can raise very personal and painful experiences (for example, see Mauthner, 1997). When they feel they trust the researcher, they sometimes use the opportunity to open up and offload many issues of concern, including child protection issues.

Young researchers conducting face to face fieldwork will need some preparation discussion and practice on how to handle the disclosure of sensitive information (⊃ see Learning Resource Materials). This should include how to talk to the respondent and bring the interview to a close if necessary, and what procedures to follow if a disclosure of abuse is made.

Within Save the Children, young researchers are instructed that they are not 'counsellors', and they should not attempt to solve respondents' problems; instead, they should refer them to another appropriate agency or worker. Young researchers are sometimes particularly concerned about the welfare of the respondents, however, and want to do something more to help than just report their experiences (e.g. Saunders and Broad, 1997) (for more information see 'Helping respondents' box). Sometimes, young researchers discuss their own related experiences with the young respondents, either during the interview or more frequently after it has finished.

Sometimes respondents also get upset when they have disclosed sensitive information (e.g. Alderson, 1995; Saunders and Broad, 1997). Young researchers have also been found to get upset by interviews in which sad or sensitive information is disclosed, or where the discussion has reminded them of their own personal and difficult experiences (e.g. Saunders and Broad, 1997). Some young

Helping respondents: *Read on if you want to know more ...*

The young researchers' empathy with young respondents possibly reflects the closer links between the peers, and raises questions about the role of the researcher to intervene and assist those they research. Oakley (1981, p. 134) cautioned professional researchers that 'in the "feminist interview", the closeness and intersubjectivity remain artificial and temporary', but where local people research within their own community then this relationship is more stable.

people may not yet have the ability to adequately deal with these issues. It is worth considering in advance what support structures might be needed for both the respondents and the young researchers to help them cope with distressing issues arising in the interviews.

- Offer respondents a debrief session after the interview (with a young researcher or worker), as recommended by The National Children's Bureau (1993), in which respondents are encouraged to discuss their experience of the research.

- Offer more worker support, including counselling if necessary. For example, in a research project about mental health needs, a counsellor attended the planning sessions in which a group of young researchers explored their personal experiences.

- Offer the young respondents or young researchers the possibility of having a friend, carer or worker close at hand (in the same or neighbouring room) to help deal with any issues that might arise.

- If the research subject is particularly sensitive, ask carers or workers whether the research might raise too many personally difficult topics for a young respondent.

- Give respondents a choice about who interviews them – including a choice of gender and ethnicity, and whether a young or adult researcher interviews them.

Confidentiality

The young researchers will need to be informed about your organisation's confidentiality policy. They often welcome the opportunity to explore what is meant by confidentiality and when it should be broken, such as in a child protection case (⊃ see Learning Resource Materials). In a study where young researchers examined leaving care issues, they felt that they had not had enough in-depth discussion on these issues (Saunders and Broad, 1997).

It is also good practice to explain confidentiality to the research respondents, and the young researchers can help to design ways of doing this. They can also benefit from rehearsing their explanation of confidentiality and answering the types of related questions respondents may ask them.

If young researchers are also research respondents – i.e. they include their personal views and experiences in the report – there is a question about whether their identity should be disguised to ensure confidentiality, in the same way that other respondents are usually protected. If this is a concern, consider the following.

- Discuss the issue with the young researchers and explain why it might be in their interest to disguise individuals' comments – as they cannot predict how others will react – particularly if they are making comments about services that they may access again in the future.

- The young researchers' names can be included on the report, but within the text the identity of who said what can be disguised.

Young people's safety

Often, the young researchers will be researching friends of friends and they may have to approach respondents they do not know. This raises a number of issues regarding the safety of the young researchers and the respondents, which are explored below.

Police checks

In the United Kingdom, where young researchers will have both 'substantial' and 'unsupervised' access to others aged under 16, it should be considered whether they need to have a police check (for example of guidance, see Home Office Circular, 1994). Police checks can take a long time to organise, and could possibly discourage some young people – including offenders and asylum seekers – from wanting to take part. Police checks are no substitute for professional vigilance and good management to help protect the young researchers and respondents.

Pair work

Sometimes, young researchers conduct their fieldwork in pairs, which provides co-support and safety. Pairing does not always work in practice, however, as the young researchers can find it hard to contact each other (particularly if they are not on the telephone) and to arrange mutually convenient times to meet.

Fieldwork location

Within Save the Children, young researchers are told not to interview in the homes of people they do not know, or not to do so on their own. They are instructed to interview in a quiet private room within a public building – such as community centres, schools, cafés (if necessary) – and to ensure they are within earshot of others so they can call for assistance if needed. Interview locations can affect what interviewees feel able to say, which may need to be given some consideration; for example, people are less likely to be critical of a GP's service if interviewed in the waiting room.

Other safety precautions

Other possible safety measures to consider are listed below. These may prove particularly necessary if the young researchers are accessing respondents on the street which raises increased protection issues.

- Workers can accompany – or remain close to – the young researchers.

- Young researchers inform workers of their movements, including when and where they conduct interviews.

- Provide mobile phones and/or personal alarms.

- Provide the young researchers with identity (ID) cards.

- Prohibit certain locations; for example, the young researchers in one study wanted to interview young people buying drugs from local dealers, but the workers decided this was too unsafe.

KEY LEARNING POINTS: Ethics

- There are a number of ethical issues that need to be considered when researching children and young people, regardless of whether the researchers are young or adults.

- There are some additional ethical issues that need to be considered when young researchers conduct research. These issues arise when there is concern that unskilled young researchers may impact negatively on other respondents.

- Decisions will need to be made about whether to access respondents through ethics committees, where they exist, or to seek alternative routes.

- The young researchers will need to be prepared to deal with the possible disclosure of sensitive information by young respondents.

- Young respondents and young researchers can become upset in interview situations. Workers need to consider what support to provide if this happens.

- Discuss with the young researchers what is meant by confidentiality, and when it should be broken. They will also need to practise how to explain confidentiality to research respondents.

- If young researchers will be interviewing people they do not know, safety precautions are needed. These can include police checks, pair work, and specifying safe fieldwork locations.

7 Dissemination and development

The dissemination strategy is key to achieving any impact from research. For those working in the field of community development, the research is just one stage in the long development process, and not an end in itself; short-term projects will rarely be as effective as long-term development strategies. The dissemination needs to be planned well in advance, allowing for the fact that it can take considerable time to present research findings and lobby for change.

Young people's involvement in dissemination

There are a number of ways in which young people can be involved in organising and carrying out the dissemination of the research findings, including the following (⊃ see Learning Resource Materials):

- identify who to send the report to (or other product)

- write accompanying letters

- distribute leaflets and posters

- write a press release

- give media interviews

- make presentations.

Research launches organised within Save the Children have usually been attended by relevant local and national professionals, and other people such as Members of Parliament, councillors, community groups, and local people; including young people, parents, and other adults. Young people can design and run the presentations alone, or with workers. The young people may choose to use imaginative ways of presenting the material, including drama, video, poetry and photography.

Presentations often include an open question and answer session, and it is here that the young researchers' level of understanding of the research process and findings becomes apparent. If the young people have not written the research report, or are not that familiar with its contents, then it can be unfair to expect them to present the research findings and answer questions on these.

The young researchers can be offered support to help present the research, in the following ways:

- presentation and media skills training

- practise their presentation and answering questions

- help with writing their presentation; the young researchers often write their own presentations, although sometimes workers have written a first draft which the young researchers then edit using their own choice of language

- workers take responsibility for parts of the presentation; for example, young researchers talk about the process whilst workers talk about the findings

- workers can answer some questions; groups signal to the workers if they would like them to answer a question – rather than the worker assuming the young people do not know the answer.

For those young people who do not enjoy public speaking, there are plenty of other tasks in which they can become involved; such as greeting delegates, compiling presentation packs, facilitating workshops, explaining displays, or using a different imaginative method of presenting the information (as discussed above).

Professionals' perspectives

When reporting the research findings of studies undertaken by young researchers, there are a number of issues that can affect how well the research is received by professionals and others, as follows.

- *Novelty.* Research undertaken by young people can help to gain publicity and attention because of the novelty value of this innovative method of consultation.

- *Setting the agenda.* Framing research questions can have as much influence as the final research findings, by raising the research issue on to the professional agenda. Involving young people also sends the clear message that they are the focus of the study; so that 'the messengers become the message' (Parry-Williams, 1998).

- *Quality Assurance.* Some professionals question the validity of research undertaken by young people, so quality assurance measures should be emphasised to external audiences in the report. Also be clear about the limitations of a piece of research (see Case study 42).

Case study 42 Residential food for young people in care

One project conducted a rigorous piece of research on food in residential care. The study used a total of seven methods to collect research data – including interviews with young people and professionals. Some social service professionals criticised the report on the grounds that the research was biased, and argued the following:

- that the views expressed in the report represented those of the young researchers – some of whom had left care a number of years before – rather than the respondents who were still in care

- the professionals' quotes were taken out of context

- the selected quotes misrepresented what was said in the text – highlighting the negative rather than positive comments about the services.

The adult academic researchers involved in the project believed that only the last of these charges might be justified. Otherwise, however, they refuted the criticisms and believed the report to offer a balanced representation of the young respondents' and adults' views. The report was also well received by a group of academic researchers who had been asked to comment on it. The workers believed the charges of bias reflected an objection to disadvantaged young people acquiring some power as researchers (Hobbiss *et al.*, 1998a, 1998b).

- *Participation improves impact.* Involving young people in the dissemination and development stages of the project can help to impact on professionals, by bringing them closer to the reality of young people's lives.

- *Professional participation.* Involving local and national professionals throughout the project – particularly those who will be instrumental in acting upon the findings and recommendations – will help to encourage them to be more committed to the outcomes of the work (see section on 'Advisory and reference groups' in Chapter 2).

Evaluating the research

An evaluation of the research project needs to be planned early on. Young people can participate by helping to set indicators, record the information and contribute their views. Decide what information is needed to measure both the research process and any impact it has. To measure the impact of the research, first establish what are the intended outcomes on services and the participating young people. It might be worth evaluating some outcomes a year or so after publication of the report, allowing it time to have an impact.

- *The research process.* The research process can be detailed and assessed, including: which groups of young people were involved, the ways in which they participated, their capacities, level of support provided, roles of workers and partner agencies, problems that arose and how these were dealt with, and any ethical considerations. Any training they receive should also be evaluated (⊃ see Learning Resource Materials).

- *Impact on policies and services.* Indicators might include any action taken, comments about the research, where it was disseminated, media coverage, presentations, invitations to conferences, planning meetings, etc., and the extent to which workers and the young people felt their comments were listened to.

- *Impact on the young researchers.* This needs to be measured against the young researchers' expectations and experience of the project, as well as the workers' hoped for outcomes. This might include their interest and enjoyment, level of participation, skills and knowledge, and future destination. (See section on 'How will young people benefit from taking part?' in Chapter 1.)

- *Impact on respondents.* The effects of the research on the interviewees can be monitored using 'debriefing' sessions (see section on 'Disclosure of sensitive information' in Chapter 6). A longitudinal review of the impacts on the respondents may also be possible if the researchers are able to return to them at a later date (see Proctor and Padfield, 1998).

Future development work with young researchers

The participatory research process creates an ideal opportunity for agencies to develop active groups of young people to work with around further policy and development issues. Young people often continue to want to be part of the group after working so intensely on a piece of work, and some groups take longer to trust workers and often require long-term support.

If there is no intention to work with the young researchers after the research has finished, this must be clearly communicated to them from the beginning of the project. This ensures they are aware there is a clear end to the project, towards which they are working, and they will not have raised expectations about what happens after it finishes. Workers should support the individuals to move on and, if the group wants to continue working together, workers can attempt to find another agency to support them.

KEY LEARNING POINTS: Dissemination and development

- A dissemination strategy is important to achieve outcomes from the research.

- Young researchers can be involved in disseminating the research findings by helping to distribute the report (and other products).

- Young researchers can also be involved in making presentations of the findings. They may need support and some presentation skills training, and workers can co-present.

- A number of issues can affect how professionals receive research undertaken by young people. For example, the novelty of participatory research will help to gain their attention, but some may require evidence of quality assurance in the research. Involving professionals in the project early on helps to build their commitment to the findings.

- An evaluation of the research project should be planned early on, and with the participation of the young researchers. It can include an evaluation of the research process, and the impact the research has on services, the young researchers and the young respondents.

- Young researchers often want to continue working as a group after the research is finished, and workers need to consider in advance what support they can offer them. If there is no intention to continue working with the young people beyond the research, they should be clearly told so.

Conclusion

Young people can take part in designing and conducting research in a number of varied ways; from simply advising adult researchers to undertaking their own research projects. They can be involved in researching the views and experiences of both young people and adults.

Careful pre-planning is needed to meaningfully involve young people in research so that it is beneficial to them, and to others whose views and experiences the research aims to represent. Forethought needs to be given first to why and how the young people are to participate. Careful consideration is then needed about whether the young researchers can be appropriately supported throughout the research process, which can be long, and their own personal development given enough attention. Different groups of young researchers will need varying levels of training and support to develop their confidence and the ability to undertake the required research tasks.

Sometimes it is inappropriate to involve young people in conducting research. The research process can be rather boring at times, and some young people may rather be involved in other types of participatory projects. The sensitivity of some research topics, and particular research contexts, can also make them unsuitable for young people to research.

Generally, this type of participatory research with young people has much to recommend itself. Young researchers have a lot to personally gain from taking part, and their involvement can benefit the research. The young researchers also have increased access to decision-making processes, which enable them to fulfil their rights as citizens to participate more fully in society.

I enjoyed the Project. It was good. I would do it again. It was good that kids got the chance to do the talking. (Young researcher, aged 14, quoted in Precht, 1998)

References

(*Essential reading)

*Alderson, P. (1995) *Listening to Children: Children, Ethics and Social Research.* London: Barnardos

Alderson, P. and Montgomery, M. (1996) *Health Care Choices: Making Decisions with Children.* London: Institute for Public Policy Research

Arber, S. (1993) 'Design samples', in N. Gilbert (ed.) *Researching Social Life.* London: Sage

Archbold, A., Davison, B., Hutton, E., Job, D., Pattison, M., Sadler, C., Thompson, E. and Wright, M. (1998) *Listen to Us: What Young People Want from a Health Service.* Newcastle: Save the Children

Article 12 Richmond (1999) *Young People, the Internet and Children's Rights* (preliminary title). London: Article 12 Richmond

Ash, A., Bellew, J., Davies, M., Newman, T. and Richardson, L. (1996) *Everybody in? The Experience of Disabled Students in Colleges of Further Education.* Ilford: Barnardos

Beresford, B. (1997) *Personal Accounts: Involving Disabled Children in Research.* Social Policy Research Unit. London: HMSO

Berridge, D. (1995) 'Involving children's centre residents in recruiting a university researcher', *Children UK*, Spring, pp. 12–13

Boldero, J. and Fallown, B. (1995) 'Adolescent help-seeking: what do they get help for and from whom?', *Journal of Adolescence,* Vol. 18, No. 2, pp. 193–209

Booth, C., Hayward, S., Jewitt, M. and Johnson, M. (1998) *Which Way Now? Young People's Experiences of Leaving Care: Researched by Young People in Hull.* London: Save the Children

*Boyden, J. and Ennew, J. (1998) *Children in Focus – a Manual for Participatory Research with Children.* Stockholm: Rädda Barnen

Chawla, L. and Kjørholt, A.T. (1996) 'Children as special citizens', *PLA Notes: Notes on Participatory Learning and Action,* No. 25, February, pp. 43–6

Connolly, M., Dougherty, C., Lavery, J., Laird, K., McCafferty, M., O Mealláin, F., Shannon, L., Tate, B. and White, D. (1996) *Out of Our Mouths, Not Out of Our Heads: A Report on Drugs and Drug Use in West Belfast Compiled by and for Young People.* Belfast: Save the Children

Coomber, R. (1997) 'Using the Internet for survey research', *Sociological Research Online,* Vol. 2, No. 2, <http://www.sociresonline.org.uk/socresonline/2/2/2.html>

Craig, D. and Porter, D. (1997) 'Framing participation: development projects, professionals, and organisations', *Development in Practice*, Vol. 7, No. 3, pp. 229–36

Curley, D. and YARD (Youth Action Research and Development) (1998) *Not Just a Place to Hang Out: The Things I would like in a Leisure Centre.* Birmingham: Save the Children

Denscombe, M. (1998) *The Good Research Guide.* Milton Keynes: Open University Press

Dent, J. (1996) 'Stumbling towards gender aware PRA training in Indonesia', *PLA Notes: Notes on Participatory Learning and Action,* No. 25, February, pp. 19–22

Educable Group (forthcoming) *Young People with Disabilities Able to be Educated* (preliminary title). Belfast: Save the Children

Fast Forward Positive Lifestyles Ltd (1994) *Drugs Information for Young People: Peer Research Project Findings.* Edinburgh: Fast Forward Positive Lifestyles Ltd

Gosling, L. and Edwards, M. (1995) *Toolkits: A Practical Guide to Assessment, Monitoring, Review and Evaluation.* SCF Development Manual 5. London: Save the Children

Hall, D.J. and Hall, I. (1996) *Practical Social Research: Project Work in the Community.* London: Macmillan

Hart, R.A. (1992) 'Children's participation; from tokenism to citizenship', *Innocenti Essays*, Vol. 4, pp. 19–22. Unicef

HAYS (Horn of Africa Youth Scheme) and Kirby, P. (1998) *Let's Spell it out: Peer Research on the Educational Support Needs of Young Refugees and Asylum Seekers living in Kensington and Chelsea.* London: Save the Children

Hill, M. (1997) 'Participatory research with children: research review', *Child and Family Social Work*, Vol. 2, pp. 171–83

Hobbiss, A., Calvert, C. and Collins, L. (1998a) 'Participative research: a way of creating research partnerships with young people', conference presentation and abstract for *Collaboration in Health Research.* Bradford: Bradford Institute for Health Research, University of Bradford

Hobbiss, A., Calvert, C., Collins, L. and Johnson, P. (1998b) *Look Ahead: Young People, Residential Care and Food.* London: Save the Children

Home Office Circular (1994) *Protection of Children: Disclosure of Criminal Background to Voluntary Sector Organisations.* HOC 42/94. London: Home Office

Howarth, R. (1997) *If we Don't Play Now, When Can we? Research into the Play and Leisure Needs of Bangladeshi Children in Camden.* London: Save the Children and Hopscotch Asian Women's Centre

Howarth, R. (forthcoming) *Report on Widening Participation in Kingsway Further Education College* (preliminary title). London: Save the Children, Hopscotch Asian Women's Centre and Kingsway College

Hurley, N. (1998) *Straight Talk: Working with Children and Young People in Groups.* Contemporary Research Issues. York: Joseph Rowntree Foundation

International Save the Children Alliance (1997) *UN Convention on the Rights of the Children Training Kit.* London: Save the Children

Johnson, V. (1996) 'Starting a dialogue on children's participation', *PLA Notes: Notes on Participatory Learning and Action,* No. 25, February, pp. 30–5

Khan, S. (1997) *Street Children's Research.* Dhaka: Save the Children

Kirby, P. and Pettitt, B. (1998) 'Evaluation of community research in the England programme' (internal report). London: Save the Children

Laws, S., Armit, D., Metzendorf, W. and Percival, P. (1999) *Time to Listen: Young People's Experiences of Mental Health Services.* Manchester: Save the Children

Macdonald, K. and Tipton, C. (1993) 'Using documents', in N. Gilbert (ed.) *Researching Social Life.* London: Sage

McDonald, L. (1996) Workshop paper presented at Save the Children conference, 'Participate research: a challenge for researchers workshop', 25 October, Belfast

McKeown, C. (1999) *Unacceptably Low: Care Leavers and Mental Health.* Newcastle: Save the Children

Mahon, A. and Glendinning, C. (1996) 'Researching children: methods and ethics', *Children & Society*, Vol. 10, No. 2, pp. 145–54

Martin, M. (1996) 'Issues of power in the participatory research process', in K. de Koning and M. Martin (eds) *Participatory Research in Health: Issues and Experiences.* Johannesburg: NPPHCN

Mauthner, M. (1997) 'Methodological aspects of collecting data from children: lessons from three research projects', *Children & Society*, Vol. 11, No. 1, pp. 16–28

Miller, J. (1996) *Never too Young – How Young Children Can Take Responsibility and Make Decisions: A Handbook for Early Years Workers.* London: The National Early Years Network and Save the Children

Miller, J. (1998) 'No fun in Bilsthorpe', *Social Action Today,* No. 7, January, pp. 9–11

*Morris, J. (1998) *Don't Leave Us Out: Involving Disabled Children and Young People with Communication Impairments.* York: Joseph Rowntree Foundation

Morrow, V. and Richards, M. (1996) 'The ethics of social research with children: an overview', *Children & Society*, Vol. 10, No. 2, pp. 90–105

Naples, N.A. (1997) 'A feminist revisiting of the insider/outsider debate: the "outsider phenomenon" in rural Iowa', in Rosanna Hertz (ed.) *Reflectivity and Voice.* London: Sage

National Children's Bureau (1993) *Guidelines for Research.* London: NCB

Neustatter, A. (1998) 'Kids, what the papers say', *The Guardian,* page 8, April

Nevison, C. (1996) *A Matter of Opinion: Research into Children and Young People's Participation Rights in the North East.* Newcastle: Save the Children

Oakley, A. (1981) 'Interviewing women', in H. Roberts *Doing Feminist Research.* London: Routledge

Okurut, S., Odong, A., Imalingat, J., Okurat, A., Oloit, L. and Oloit, F. (1996) 'Participatory research processes and empowerment: the PACODET community, Uganda', in K. de Koning and M. Martin (eds) *Participatory Research in Health: Issues and Experiences.* Johannesburg: NPPHCN

Oldham, J. (1998) 'The needs of young people in Spon End: researching the social and leisure needs' (internal paper). Birmingham: Save the Children

Olesen, V. (1998) 'Feminism and models of qualitative research', in N. Denzin and Y. Lincoln (eds) *The Landscapes of Qualitative Research: Theories and Issues.* London: Sage

Parry-Williams, J. (1998) *Evaluation, Primarily by Children Evaluators, on the SCF (UK) Female-headed Project, Tajikstan.* Tajikstan: Save the Children

Pettitt, B. (ed.) (1998) *Children and Work in the UK: Reassessing the Issues.* London: CPAG and Save the Children

Precht, D. (1998) *The Paradise Project; Children's Research on Tourism in Grenada.* Grenada: Save the Children

*Pretty J.N., Guijt, I., Scoones, I. and Thompson, J. (1995) *A Trainer's Guide for Participatory Learning and Action.* IIED Participatory Methodology Series. London: IIED

Proctor, I. and Padfield, M. (1998) 'The effect of the interview on the interviewee', *International Journal of Social Research Methodology: Theory and Practice,* Vol. 1, No. 2, pp. 123–36

Saunders, L. and Broad, R. (1997) *The Health Needs of Young People Leaving Care.* Leicester: Centre for Social Action, De Montfort University

Save the Children (1996) *Round Our End: A Photography Project by Year 6 Pupils.* Newcastle: Save the Children

Save the Children Staff Workshop (1998) *Working with Young Researchers* (internal report). London: Save the Children

Save the Children and Whitley Abbey School (1999) *Report on Pupil Participation in Whitley Abbey School* (preliminary title). Birmingham: Save the Children

Schwandt, T.A. (1998) 'Constructivist, interpretivist approaches to human inquiry', in N. Denzin and Y. Lincoln (eds) *The Landscapes of Qualitative Research: Theories and Issues*. London: Sage

Sellers, T. and Westerby, M. (1996) 'Teenage facilitators: barriers to improving adolescent sexual health', *PLA Notes: Notes on Participatory Learning and Action,* No. 25, February, pp. 77–80

Stanfield, J.H. (1998) 'Ethnic modelling in qualitative research', in N. Denzin and Y. Lincoln (eds) *The Landscapes of Qualitative Research: Theories and Issues*. London: Sage

Trinder, L. (1996) 'Social work research: the state of the art (or science)', *Child and Family Social Work*, Vol. 1, pp. 233–42

UNICEF (1995) *The United Nations Convention on the Rights of the Child*. London: UNICEF

Ward, L. (1997) *Seen and Heard: Involving Disabled Children and Young People in Research and Development Projects*. York: Joseph Rowntree Foundation

Webber, S. and Longhurst, K. (forthcoming) 'Youth perceptions of citizenship and security in Russia, Germany and the UK' (research project name), School of Social Studies Centre for Russian and East Eastern European Studies, University of Birmingham, <http://www.bham.ac.uk/cmil/>

West, A. (1997) 'Participation and attitude: young people, research and dissemination' (unpublished paper). Leeds: Save the Children

Westcott, H.L. and Davies, G.M. (1995) 'Children's help-seeking behaviour', *Child: Care Health and Development,* Vol. 21, No. 4, pp. 255–70

Woodward, D. and Chisholm, L. (1981) 'The expert's view?', in H. Roberts *Doing Feminist Research.* London: Routledge

Worrall, S. (2000) *Young People as Researchers: A Learning Resource Pack.* London: Save The Children

YARD and Oldham, J. (1998a) *YARD Newsletter Report.* Birmingham: Save the Children

YARD and Oldham, J. (1998b) *A Day in the Life: Peer Research Looking at the Views and Support Needs of Permanently Excluded Young People throughout the City of Coventry.* Birmingham: Save the Children